DISRUPTIONS
NAVIGATING THE UNEXPECTED

Aaron j Robinson

Disruptions: Navigating the Unexpected
Aaron j Robinson
Published by VintageImage Press
P.O. Box 430351, Pontiac, MI 48343

Copyright © 2021 **Vintage**Image **Press**
IMAGINE • INSCRIBE • INSPIRE

Paperback ISBN 978-1-7376650-0-7

Digital (ebook) ISBN 978-1-7376650-1-4

Library of Congress Control Number: 2021915632

All rights reserved. No part of this publication may be reproduced, stored in a retrieval system, or transmitted in any form or by any means, such as electronically, photocopied, or digitally recorded, without the prior written permission of the publisher. Brief quotations in printed reviews and scholarly publications allowed.

Abbreviations:

BDAG	*A Greek-English Lexicon of the New Testament and Other Early Christian Literature.*
Louw and Nida	*Greek-English Lexicon of the New Testament: Based on Semantic Domains.*
NIDOTTE	*New International Dictionary of Old Testament Theology & Exegesis.*

Unless otherwise noted, all Scripture quotations are taken from the *NEW AMERICAN STANDARD BIBLE®*, Copyright © 1960, 1962, 1963, 1971, 1972, 1973, 1975, 1977, 1995 by The Lockman Foundation. Used by permission.

TO MY QUEEN, KAREN,
AND MY CHILDREN; AARON II, ISAIAH, JEREMIAH, KENNEDY, AND KHARIS:
THANK YOU FOR YOUR LOVE, HONOR, AND SUPPORT THROUGH
EVERY ***DISRUPTION*** WE HAVE NAVIGATED.

CONTENTS

INTRODUCTION	7
1 DEMARCATION: WHERE DO YOU STAND?	13
THE MAKER AND THE MASTER	13
A MESS AND A MASTERPIECE	23
THE OLD TWENTY DOLLAR BILL BIT...	43
QUESTIONS FOR REFLECTION	45
2 DEFINITION: WHAT IS GOING ON?	46
AN INTERRUPTION OR DISRUPTION?	46
A 'DIVINE' INTERRUPTION?	54
DISRUPTIONS ARE 'THINGS'	64
WHAT ARE YOU DOING?	67
QUESTIONS FOR REFLECTION	68
3 DELAY: WHAT ARE YOU WAITING FOR?	69
WAITING ON THE WORLD TO CHANGE	69
WAITING ON GOD: THE EXAMPLES	75
THEY THAT WAIT: THE EXERCISE OF WAITING	79
A RENEWED STRENGTH: THE EFFECT OF WAITING	83
MOUNT, RUN, WALK: THE EVIDENCE OF WAITING	85
WHAT ARE YOU WAITING FOR?	90
QUESTIONS FOR REFLECTION	92
4 DEATH: WHAT ARE YOU SAYING?	93
OH BROTHER, THIS IS BAD!	96
PREACHERS & PALLBEARERS	99
CAN THESE DRY BONES LIVE?	107

WHAT ARE YOU SAYING?	112
QUESTIONS FOR REFLECTION	114
5 DERAILMENT: WHAT ARE YOU THINKING?	**115**
CONDUCTORS AND CATASTROPHES	117
THE KING, THE CART, AND THE CATASTROPHE	119
WHEN GOD BREAKS THROUGH	123
REALIGNMENT: GETTING BACK ON TRACK	125
WHAT ARE YOU THINKING?	131
QUESTIONS FOR REFLECTION	133
6 DESTINY: WHAT ARE YOU AIMING FOR?	**134**
GOING FOR GOALS, NOT GOLD!	134
RULES AND REGULATIONS	137
THERE'S NO 'PLACE' LIKE HOME!	141
FROM THEORY TO APPLIED THEOLOGY	144
ON YOUR MARK | GETTING IN PLACE	146
GET SET | GETTING IN POSITION	152
GO | GOING FOR THE PRIZE	153
WHAT ARE YOU AIMING FOR?	157
QUESTIONS FOR REFLECTION	158
7 CONCLUSION: WHERE DO WE START?	**159**
CLOSING PRAYER	162
BIBLIOGRAPHY	**163**
ABOUT THE AUTHOR	**167**

INTRODUCTION

Most of us have days that are forever etched in our memory. We can probably relive those days so vividly that we could tell you what clothes we were wearing. For some, those days can be exciting days. For others, those days might be painful or fearful memories. One of those days for me was March 10, 2020. Several weeks prior to that date I had heard the term 'Corona Virus,' but it was something in another country; it had nothing to do with us here in the United States. In March, however, that reality changed. The virus had come what we call 'state-side.' And now, on March 10, it finally hit home.

Two cases had been discovered in the state of Michigan; both were in the counties where I minister. Shortly after the announcement made the news, the governor of Michigan made a declaration that schools would be closed down for the next three weeks. Due to its severity, her goal was to prevent the spread of the virus, for which there was no cure. Our ministry serves children in the inner-cities of Detroit and Pontiac; if the schools were not meeting, wisdom says we should follow the lead.

Talk about a **_DISRUPTION_**! We had plans...BIG PLANS! We had plans for both spiritual and numerical growth in our ministry. We had children that were anxiously waiting to enter our teen leadership program. We were only a few weeks into an exciting sixteen-week semester! We had a team of interns coming in later that month to check out our ministry. The Power Company Kids Club was on its way to developing a new urban ministry internship program.

What was initially a three-week break would become a sixteen month long hiatus for our ministry. Our state was under a mandated shelter-in-place order from the governor. Our organization ministers to children and families in one of our nation's hotbeds of outbreak. Power Company visits nearly 1,400 children in their homes in Detroit and Pontiac every week. This new shelter-in-place order brought that to a screeching halt. Our visitation ministry became phone calls, text messages, and social media only.[1] Our Saturday program, for which our fleet of fourteen former school buses would

---

[1] Although we had been doing this already; now this was the sole way of connecting with our families.

drive all over the cities picking up kids and bring them to our gym... paused until the summer of 2021... and the list goes on.

Those were just the ministry **DISRUPTIONS**. Personally, I was only one year into my doctoral studies, and was looking forward to the annual meeting of my cohorts at Bangor University, convening at the Center of Pentecostal Theology in Tennessee. That meeting was now reduced to a Zoom conference. My middle son was celebrating his eighteenth birthday in just a couple of weeks. He had been planning what this day would be like for quite a while. **DISRUPTED**. The closest that he got to a party with friends was a long day on Fortnite. Besides a lockdown order, his friends didn't have access to transportation like the cool 'drive-by' stories that were so popular on the news. My daughter turned three the day before his birthday. Ok, who am I kidding... a three-year-old birthday party can *hardly* be disrupted...my wife baked her a cake, and that was that!

My son was also in his senior year of high school. It's enough that he was homeschooled and that some of the nostalgia that came along with senior memories would already be different. Now for him and every other class of 2020 student in the country, even a commencement service, which he would have participated in with other home schoolers, was off the table. He had worked so hard at finishing strong. His grind was REAL! But... **DISRUPTION!**

There were other major challenges in our family. My younger sister would turn 40 in just two short weeks. While she had the maturity to understand that she might not be able to 'turn up' this year, it was no ordinary birthday. She was a little over a year in remission from cancer, and just a couple of months before all of this she found out that the cancer was back. She would begin chemotherapy rounds for the second time... *on her birthday!* Now THAT is a **DISRUPTION**! Instead of the big birthday bash that was planned months earlier, her party consisted of me, my wife, and my children standing outside the window of her house playing 'Hallelujah, Today My Birthday!' by Crash Cut.[2]

On the other side of town, another one of my younger sisters was giving birth to her first child. Now, I know that there are hundreds of thousands of women that experience this iconic moment without being

---

[2] No, there was not a typo here. These are the words to the song. Do yourself a favor and search it out on YouTube... You're welcome!

surrounded by family. But she is the baby of the family and had navigated her entire pregnancy anticipating certain things. She wanted to welcome her child into the world surrounded by aunts, uncles, cousins, and more. No one except she and her husband were allowed in the hospital. He was not permitted to leave to go buy her a non-hospital meal, post-delivery... **DISRUPTION**! As I write these words, I have not yet met my handsome nephew.

Friends have lost jobs. Some thriving ministries began losing support. Some churches, unable to grab hold of the technology reins, had to close their doors. Many lost faithful members to online ministries with more charismatic preachers. **DISRUPTION**! The economy suffered, the ministry suffered, families suffered, and the first responders committed to trying to keep our communities safe suffered. It was so bad that even Teddy Riley suffered in his Instagram Live music battle against Baby Face...hey, if you missed it, you missed it!

It wasn't until a conversation with one of the leaders in our ministry that the Lord began to turn my attention to Scripture, and really look at a Biblical way to handle disruptions. Ramon and I met regularly before the pandemic, and we decided to keep the momentum and meet online. He shared with me how the pandemic had impacted him, and that it was a major **DISRUPTION** for him. I did not realize then that I was also speaking to myself, launching into a Biblical study that would radically transform the way that I looked at disruptions. I asked Ramon frankly, *'What are you doing!?'* I warned him that his daily disciplines during this unprecedented time had dramatic implications on his future. Simply put, I asked him, *'We will come out of this...and what then?'* As our discussion progressed, I explained to him that this could be a defining moment for him in ministry and life in general.

After that conversation, Ramon asked if I would be sharing deeper on the topic at our next Sunday morning Bible study. Hmmm...maybe I should! And I did. Week after week, people began to join us for this discussion. I thought that I would blog about it until Chris Palmer, a friend and fellow Bangor scholar texted me one day and encouraged me to write a book. That text was an hour before I sat down to write this introduction. Three months later, I closed the final chapter.

This book is not my *Covid Chronicles*. It's not a book on *Faith Over Fear*. In fact, you can probably take any super-spiritual, hyper-faith, over-tweeted theme, and tell yourself, *"This is not that!"* True, the COVID-19 pandemic was a catalyst to the conversation with which I hope to engage you over the next several chapters, but it is not the focus.[3] COVID-19 was a global disruption, but the reality is all of us face disruptions in our lives. Unfortunately, there were millions of people already in a private **DISRUPTION** of their own before any pandemic.

When we are facing disruptions, there are so many questions we want to ask, and so many we want to hear asked of us. *'Whose fault is this!?' 'When will this end?!' How are you doing?' 'What do you need?'* These questions seem to offer solace in our time of uncertainty. Good questions. Valid questions. But not necessarily forward-moving questions. We should ask these questions, but the main question we need to be asking ourselves is, *'What am I doing?'* Our actions, in the midst of a disruption, help determine the outcome. This is not a message of prosperity, although I pray it brings hope to the reader. Rather, it is a message of perspective and priority. It is not about favor over fear, but faithfulness in fearful times.

Sometimes when I am reading books, I have the tendency to scan over the table of contents and jump to the chapters that seem to matter most to me. There are many books that are written to be read that way such as reference and recipe books: they are organized by essays or themes. This book does not fall into such a category. I encourage you not to approach this book that way. I recommend starting at the very first chapter and taking the journey with me. In the first chapter, I address two views that are often distorted. It is my belief that oftentimes some of the disruptions we face have much to do with these views, and less to do with external circumstances. The views that I am speaking of are our view of God and our view of ourselves. As we navigate through chapter 1, I hope to help you see that when these views are Biblically aligned, many of our disruptions can be avoided.

In the second chapter, I aim to bring definition to this topic, disruption. I've given a few examples of disruptions already, but perhaps you don't identify with the disruptions that I have mentioned. This will not be a long chapter that explains why God allows suffering, or why bad things happen to good people. Those are very important topics, and I don't think they can be fully answered in one chapter. However, it is important for this

---

[3] Admittedly, COVID-19 makes for a good conversation partner, as it is a disruption that most readers would be familiar with, to some degree. Therefore, the topic does come up from time to time, only to help illustrate a point.

work to offer a quick glance at why disruptions even take place, if not for a distorted view of God and ourselves. In the chapters to follow, I intend to present to you four possible outcomes to a disruption,[4] and show you the actions that get us there. I will also give Biblical examples and instructions by which we can change course and move closer to what God intends for us, in the midst of any disruption. Along this journey, I will share personal stories, engage with various authors who I think do an amazing job making my point clearer, and try my best to be extremely practical, and not too philosophical about how we handle disruptions. At the end of each chapter, I encourage you to interact with the discussions. You might even grab a partner to join you in this study, especially a spouse.

---

[4] I admit, there are certainly more outcomes, but these four are what I have experienced, both in my own life, and over two decades of ministry leadership. As you follow along, I believe you will find this list agreeably familiar.

Before we turn our attention to the first chapter, let us consider first our presuppositions and preconceived notions about disruptions. Let's call this the pre-test. We will visit these questions again, but first let's just get some waypoint markers on the map. Don't spend long engaging these questions; answer them as quickly and as honestly as you can.

1. List your top 3 memorable disruptions.

2. What questions did you ask the most?

3. Which of these questions helped you to progress?

4. From which of these disruptions did you come out better or stronger than before?[5]

Now, let's navigate together!

AaronjRob

---

[5] Notice the question: better, stronger... not bitter, harder. Some tend to think that better and stronger means bigger, thicker walls, lower expectations or aversion to steps of faith. This is the opposite of better and stronger.

1 DEMARCATION: WHERE DO YOU STAND?

THE MAKER AND THE MASTER

> **Genesis 1:1–2 (NASB)**
> In the beginning God created the heavens and the earth. The earth was formless and void, and darkness was over the surface of the deep, and the Spirit of God was moving over the surface of the waters.
>
> **John 1:1–2 (NASB)**
> In the beginning was the Word, and the Word was with God, and the Word was God. He was in the beginning with God.

If everything started with God, it would be silly to start this book in any other way. Besides, it is our view(s) about God that get most of us tripped up in our disruption seasons anyway. Whether you are reading this book as a Christian, or an atheist/anti-theist, or your faith/belief system falls somewhere on the spectrum in between, one inescapable reality is that our view of God informs our view of disruptions. Let us consider some of the various views of God, and how those views can inform the challenges that we experience in life. We will start from the outer perimeter (there is no God), and work our way inward (belief in the God of Scripture), and you will notice that even devout Christians can have a distorted view of God, and thus come out of their disruptions scathed, bruised, and broken.

THE ANTI-THEIST: THERE IS NO GOD.

Can anyone *really* say that there is no God? According to Ray Comfort, "For the statement to be true, I must know for certain that there is no God in the entire universe. No human being has all knowledge; therefore, none of us is able to truthfully make this assertion."[6] But some find it difficult to believe in God; specifically, the God of Scripture, and there are

---

[6] Ray Comfort, God Doesn't Believe in Atheists: Proof That the Atheist Doesn't Exist (Orlando, FL: Bridge-Logos Publishers, 1993), 15.

varying reasons as to why.[7] D.A. Carson writes that "Even those who were atheists were, shall I say, *Christian* atheists. That is to say, the God they disbelieved in was the God of the Bible. Their understanding of the God whom they found unbelievable was in some measure shaped by their reading of the Bible."[8] It has been said that anti-theists believe that "scientific facts describe the real nature of the world, and are therefore the key to progress, while values and religious beliefs are mere human inventions—at best unnecessary options but perhaps harmful superstitions."[9] Anti-theists hold various beliefs, all of which we cannot cover here, but they can range from atheists (no god), to agnostics (highly doubt, need hard evidence to prove it), and evolutionists (science is my god).[10]

The point here is not to debate the issue of the existence of God; rather, it is to consider how such a view of a world without God might impact the way we navigate through disruptions of life. If you believe that there is no God, in essence your belief system or worldview is one that suggests that you or science are in ultimate control. There's no such thing as karma, there's no God, the 'universe' isn't upset, and even sowing and reaping should be taken off the table because this suggests that there is some divine being with a system of moral balances, that keeps good and evil in continuous play against one another. Therefore, for the anti-theist a disruption can be nothing more or nothing less than an inconvenient season of life that they just have to navigate. This view might afford the anti-theist the ability to approach disruptions without a totally defeated mindset. They can look at a disruption with optimism that life may simply continue beyond what they are currently facing.

On the other hand, and probably more likely, an anti-theist worldview is void of a sense of purpose. Whatever happens, regardless the crisis… well, it just happens… *es lo que es* (it is what it is) … *que sera sera*

---

[7] See John M. Frame, "Why It Seems So Difficult Today to Believe in Christianity," in *Christianity Considered: A Guide for Skeptics and Seekers*, ed. Todd Hains, Mark L. Ward Jr., and Elizabeth Vince (Bellingham, WA: Lexham Press, 2018), 9-13, for a brief explanation on these reasons.

[8] D. A. Carson, *The God Who Is There: Finding Your Place in God's Story* (Grand Rapids, MI: Baker Books, 2010), 11.

[9] Jonathan Clatworthy, Making Sense of Faith in God: How Belief Makes Science Possible (London: SPCK, 2012), 7.

[10] See "Anti-Theistic Theories," in Paul Ennis, *The Moody Handbook of Theology, Revised and Expanded* (Chicago, IL: Moody Publishers, 1989), 191.

(whatever will be will be). Such a view of life can be overwhelming, depending on the disruption that you're facing. I can imagine that such a view has led some people to look at life as utterly hopeless, as this is simply 'the hand they were dealt.' Some have devoted their scholarship and research to disproving the existence of God and dismantling the institution of religion.[11] Disruptions (suffering and evil) can play a major role in the acceptance of there being a God.

THE RELIGIOUS: THERE IS A GOD (OR GODS)

Not all find it difficult to believe in God. For some, the challenge is not believing in a god or gods; it is believing solely in the God of Scripture. While Muslims and non-messianic Jews believe in one God and Creator, the rejection of the triune God of the Bible (Father, Son, Spirit), leads me to include them in the following category. I will admit that this section would be a very broad stroke of the brush! I agree with David W. Shenk, who says that "it is impossible to fully understand the perceptions of another's faith system."[12]

Let's start wide and then narrow our belief parameters. In this category, you have two choices; one God, or many gods. The many gods view itself has two major categories: polytheism, which means there are *many* gods, and pantheism, which means that *everything* is god, and god is everything.[13] This might sound familiar if you have a keen knowledge of Bible narratives, and you recall the children of Israel, and their time in Egypt, and engagements with nations in the land of Canaan. How many times were they warned against worshipping idols? Even in the New Testament, Paul pointed out that the men of Athens worshipped *many* gods that were hand-made (Acts 17).

What is the inherent problem of making many, or all things a god? Men have written books on the matter, so to avoid trying to sound like an apologist (a person who is pretty good at debating and arguing for the existence of God), I would refer to the authors that I have quoted thus far.

---

[11] See Alister McGrath, *Why God Won't Go Away: Engaging with the New Atheism* (London: SPCK, 2011), for more on a few modern authors, and their work that has been aimed at disproving and dismantling.

[12] David W. Shenk, *Global Gods: Exploring the Role of Religions in Modern Societies* (Scottdale, PA: Herald Press, 1995), 37.

[13] For more on these views, see Ennis, *Moody Handbook*, 192.

However, there are some points that I want to turn our attention to as it pertains to disruptions: outlook, ownership, and optimism.

Many gods, or everything a god, makes the view blurry, in the midst of a disruption. Consider the 2011 movie, Real Steel, with Hugh Jackman. The short story is that a once-great boxer who now gambles on robot fights, finds out that he has a son who comes to live with him for the summer. His son finds a robot (Atom) that can mimic the movement of his controller. Pause and think 'mechanical Rocky Balboa,' so that I can skip to the end. Atom fights his way up the robot circuit to finally make it to the big show... a championship fight with the undefeated Zeus.

At a certain point in this championship bout, Atom experiences a disruption. He gets the terabytes knocked out of him by Zeus. Suddenly, the remote mechanisms don't work anymore, and Jackman is unable to direct Atom's movements with the remote-control joysticks. Jackman does what EVERY SINGLE PERSON watching the movie knew he was going to do. Jackman throws down the controller, puts on a headset, and says to Atom, *"Look at me! Focus on me!"* And Atom looks for the person wearing the headset. When he has him in sight... you guessed it. He mimics Jackman's moves, ducking, dodging, jabbing, upper-cutting, bobbing and weaving, until he finally knocks Zeus down. Only saved by the ringing of the bell, Zeus won the match. His victory was only a formality of points. Ultimately, it was Atom who was crowned 'the people's champion.'

So, back to our 'many gods' issue. When we are facing our 'Zeus' disruptions, who is wearing the headset? Who are we to look to? Could you imagine how differently that match would have gone if ten other boxers stood around the ring with a headset saying "Watch me! Focus on ME!"? Better yet, put a headset on everyone in the stadium! Atom would have gone into a frenzy, and gotten mangled! And that is precisely what happens to some people who have placed hope in many gods, or they have mistakenly believed that god is everything and everything is god. I guess we should have defined that term from the jump, but I think we're on the same page, *right?!*

GOD = ULTIMATE AUTHORITY!

If 'the one who has ultimate authority' is our definition of God, then a polytheist or pantheist view suggests that many things, or *everything* can tell me how to best navigate uncertain situations. At best, we fall into the same trappings as the anti-theist, with the resolve that we are our own god. We have the ultimate authority here. At worst, we take that view a step further and feel that if we cannot control this current disruption, then the disruption, or the circumstances causing the disruption have the ultimate authority. Our fate is sealed in our circumstances.

So, let's say there is just one God. That is good enough, right?! As stated above, Muslims and (non-messianic) Jews believe that there is one God (as do Christians), but they reject the notion of the incarnation of Jesus as Messiah, a clear point of division. There is also deism, which believes in God, but believes that he is too far removed from his creation (transcendent) to step into matters that concern his creation (immanent).[14] It is great that we can all agree that there is one God, but, as Timothy Keller notes, "we couldn't all be equally right about the nature of God."[15] Non-Christian *monotheistic* (one God only) religions might fall into what Keller calls a 'moral improvement' category of religions, which (broadly speaking) promises heaven or paradise as a reward for living a good (moral) life.[16] Some have characterized this form of belief as a religion based on *legalism.* These religions are steeped in laws. But doesn't Christianity have laws, or codes of conduct to live by? Legalism can be a problem in Christianity as well (a point we will consider later).

The problem of laws without a Lamb (oops...spoiler alert) is the fact that they can create false reads for us when we are in a disruption. One false read (which exists in Christianity as well), is to equate our disruptions to some neglect of a moral law. In other words, disruption = disobedience. Sometimes, that is an accurate interpretation of events, but not always. Some disruptions are not because we did wrong...but let's not get there quite yet. Secondly, these religions offer no *ultimate* hope beyond our disruption.

Now to be fair, if you are not a Christian, you might have read all that I just wrote and feel as though I am missing something. There is a great chance that I have. My attempt was not to offer a deep survey of religions, but just offer a helicopter view of how non-Christian belief systems (also

---

[14] Ennis, *Moody Handbook*, 745.
[15] Timothy Keller, The Reason for God: Belief in an Age of Skepticism (New York: Penguin, 2009) 55.
[16] Keller, *The Reason for God,* 82. Keller does not specifically mention these religions, but the general point that he makes would include Muslim and Jewish religions.

called *worldviews*) might impact our perspective when facing a disruption. The common denominator in all of the previously mentioned views is simply that they all have displaced Jesus. Even in a pantheistic view that says he is God, the problem is the same worldview says that Timber, our family's old rescue dog, is just as much God. Houston, we have a problem.

It can seem too weak an argument, too cliché a claim, but truly Jesus does make the difference. Without Jesus, our hope amid a disruption is limited. Our ultimate hope, beyond this disruption-filled life, doesn't even exist. Some might argue that we have absolutely no hope amid a disruption apart from Jesus. But, let me explain what is meant by *limited hope*. What I mean is that we can find partial or temporary relief from our current disruptions, apart from Jesus. Unfortunately, those lead to further disruptions and greater needs for Jesus. Ask anyone suffering an addiction. We need Jesus!

THE CHRISTIAN: ONE GOD (FATHER, SON, HOLY SPIRIT)

Ahh!! FINALLY! Now we're getting somewhere! And then there's us! Now wait! Before you Christian readers begin humming, rocking, and preparing to tune up the 'Amens', we have to acknowledge the Christian's distorted view(s) of God. Even the views noted here, are not comprehensive. I just seek to point out that we have some problems as well when it comes to our view of God. As with non-Christian religions, the spectrum within Christianity is quite wide. Here, I do not seek to address Roman Catholic versus Protestant, denominationalism, church doctrines such as Reformed, Pentecostalism, Baptist, etc. I will not discuss tradition here. I simply want to point out that even when you add Jesus into the equation, it doesn't mean your view of God is correct. In fact, consider N.T. Wright's excellently stated opinion here:

> Plenty of people in the church and outside it have made up a 'Jesus' for themselves, and have found that this invented character makes few real demands on them. He makes them feel happy from time to time, but doesn't challenge them, doesn't suggest they get up and do something about

the plight of the world. Which is, of course, what the real Jesus had an uncomfortable habit of doing.[17]

That is just one end of the scale. True, some have relegated Jesus to their religious snuggie… you know that hideous Netflix blanket…that you keep tucked in a basket until you're cold and want to cuddle up to a bingeful weekend of 24 or some other great show. But there's also the other side of the scale. There is the WWJD crew! You remember the bracelets, bumper stickers, and all sorts of other swag, posing the ever so popular question, *'What would Jesus do?'* Well, it's not that difficult. If we read the gospels and Acts, we'd see just what he did.

But that's not what we're asking, right? We are asking what he would do if he were in our shoes. But as Wright also says, "Christianity is not about Jesus offering a wonderful moral example, as though our principal need was to see what a life of utter love and devotion to God and to other people would look like, so that we could try to copy it."[18] Some have reduced Christianity to a moral game of *follow the leader*. Now, don't get me wrong, we are taught by Scripture to have the mind of Christ (Philippians 2:5), but that is not the sum of the gospel. Christianity is not merely what we can do *like* Jesus, but it is first who we are *because of* Jesus and *in Jesus* (1 Corinthians 1:30, what we are able to do *through* Jesus (Philippians 4:13), and *for* (as representatives of) Jesus (Colossians 3:17).

Another major misconception of Jesus is our freedom in Jesus. John Stott called freedom a 'great Christian word,' and says that "Jesus Christ is portrayed in the New Testament as the world's supreme liberator."[19] And he is right! Jesus said that freedom was his agenda (Luke 4:18). He even boasted in being quite good at achieving his goal, basically claiming that if he set us free, we are *absolutely* free! (John 8:36). The apostle Paul must have been convinced of this, because when he wrote to the church in Galatia he encouraged them that Christ set us free so that we might actually

---

[17] N. T. Wright, *Following Jesus: Biblical Reflections on Discip*leship (London: Society for Promoting Christian Knowledge, 1994), ix.

[18] Tom Wright, *Simply Christian* (London: Society for Promoting Christian Knowledge, 2006), 78.

[19] John Stott, *Why I Am a Christian* (Nottingham, England: Inter-Varsity Press, 2003), 86.

experience freedom (Galatians 5:1). And to the Romans, he wrote that we have been set free from the law of sin and death (Romans 8:2).

But unfortunately, some have not really understood what to do with that freedom. I consider myself a fairly wise dad. I mean, I am probably the reason my father lost his hair at such a young age, so I figured I'd make sure my sons did not give me the same problems. Lying, stealing, laziness, the whole nine; that was young Aaron. This was before the advent of cell phones, much less *smartphones*. We didn't have the internet when I was growing up. Heck, I purchased my first computer after I was married for a couple years. My sons were all homeschooled, so there was really no need for my sons to have cellphones, but when they started getting summer jobs, and Karen and I did more traveling, we decided it was time. Even still, what they wanted and what they needed were two different things.

One thing I love about Apple devices is the parental control that they offer! My sons all had Macs and iPads for their homeschool learning, and we finally caved in and got the oldest two iPhones. Thank you, Jesus, for Craigslist! While other kids thought it was cool that my kids had these gadgets, my sons thought otherwise. They might as well have had Jitterbug devices. You know, the big button senior citizen cell phone they would advertise on TV? The reason is, I had parental restrictions turned on EVERYTHING! I limited which apps they could access, which websites they could navigate. If I could have put a parental control on how bright the screen got, then I probably would have.

I'll never forget when Aaron (AJ) was nearing his eighteenth birthday. 'Uh, Dad…' he asked, 'am I going to still have to have restrictions on my phone when I turn eighteen, because I will technically be an adult, and I think that would look a little silly if my dad is controlling whether or not I can surf the web or something.' Now, since he had come to me in such a mature way, I was willing to entertain the question. 'AJ, what would you do if restrictions were lifted? Why is it ultimately important to you?' He was honest. He wanted a social media account, but vowed that he wouldn't be on the phone all the time. And sometimes, he may just need to ask Google something! Point taken. And well, even without him asking, Karen and I had already decided that it would be a little juvenile to keep restrictions on his phone at that age, having graduated high school.

Not even thirty days after his birthday, it seemed like my son grew a long skinny tail. He went to the store and purchased an extra-long charging cable. He was on his phone so much that the battery wouldn't last a day! 'Aaron! What happened to not being on social media all day?!' Well, I was not prepared for his response, but I should have seen it coming... 'I'm not on social media... I'm playing a game.' As my sons would say... *'Got'em!'* Oh, the look on his face too... like he just schooled me. Eventually he became ridiculously connected to his phone, having a notification for just about every game, every post, and listening to his music. We had to have a sit-down to explain the purpose of removing restrictions. We wanted him to be free to do what was ethically, morally, and responsibly necessary and/or appropriate. Not that games are bad, but too much of anything makes you an addict (wait...90's song?).

This is also true for our freedom in Christ. It does not mean that we live life without filters. Quite the opposite. Being a part of the body of Christ demands something of our lives more than unbridled living and moral apathy. Consider what Peter instructs believers.

> **1 Peter 1:13–17 (NASB)**
>
> [13] Therefore, prepare your minds for action, keep sober in spirit, fix your hope completely on the grace to be brought to you at the revelation of Jesus Christ. [14] As obedient children, do not be conformed to the former lusts which were yours in your ignorance, [15] but like the Holy One who called you, be holy yourselves also in all your behavior; [16] because it is written, "YOU SHALL BE HOLY, FOR I AM HOLY." [17] If you address as Father the One who impartially judges according to each one's work, conduct yourselves in fear during the time of your stay on earth.

Stott explains the point of our freedom very well; that we are both free *from* and free *for*. We are free from guilt, judgment, and "the cramping bondage of our own self-centeredness."[20] It is what we are free *for* that excites me the most. Every created being is ultimately limited from *absolute* freedom, simply as a matter of created capacity (meaning, I am not free to fly... unless it's on an aircraft). However, Stott is right in suggesting that "true freedom is freedom to be one's true self, as God made us and meant us

---

[20] Stott, *Why I am a Christian*, 88-89.

to be."[21] The freedom that we have in Christ is not so that we can do whatever our current state of emotions, state of affairs, or popular culture tells us that we can. Christ has made us free so that we would, as I have heard it said, '*Live our best life!*' I know it seems like we have taken a detour from disruptions; but, this connects.

How we view Jesus is everything when it comes to disruptions. Far too often, we restrict faith in Jesus to the third chapter of John's gospel… (3:14), thus never experiencing the beauty of Jesus, the good shepherd who came that we would experience life, 'and that more abundantly' (10:10). In other words, it is great to have an ultimate hope in Jesus, as I alluded to earlier, but a true *Biblical* view of life in Christ is so much more! Unfortunately, some have distorted what that *so much more* looks like. We ought to be careful that we don't make Christianity out to be a lottery ticket religion, or genie bottle belief system. There is, however, a *fullness of life* that we should expect to experience when we put our hope and trust in Jesus. THAT makes all the difference in the world when we encounter disruptions. *WAIT! How can you have fullness of life AND disruptions… something doesn't add up.* Many people struggle with this question, which we will certainly address in the next chapter.

Since "the first place to begin in trying to understand what Christianity is, and who Jesus is, is to start again to read the Bible,"[22] let us conclude this section with a brief consideration of what a Biblical view of God would be. How has God revealed himself to us in Scripture? Consider the following Bible passages, and what they tell us about God, his nature, his character, and his activity in our world; more specifically, in our lives.[23] This list is not even close to exhaustive, but it does begin to set a foundation for our thinking about God, and how aligning our view of him with the Bible might help us better navigate disruptions.

---

[21] Stott, *Why I am a Christian*, 94.
[22] Carson, *The God Who Is There*, 11.
[23] Adopted from Carson, *The God Who Is There*; and R. C. Sproul, *What Can We Know about God?*. First edition, Vol. 27, The Crucial Questions Series (Orlando, FL: Reformation Trust, 2017).

- God was and is… he was not created. (Genesis 1:1)
- God is one in nature. (Deuteronomy 6:4-5)
- God coequally exists as three distinct persons; Father, Son, Spirit. (John 14:26)
- God is our creator and our sustainer. (Genesis 1; Acts 17:28)
- God is worthy of our praise. (Psalm 150:6)
- God the Son (Jesus) is our model for living. (Ephesians 5:1-2)
- God speaks. (Genesis 1:3)
- God doesn't make mistakes (only good things). (Genesis 1-2)
- God is Holy. (Leviticus 11:44; 1 Peter 1:16)
- God loves, and he is love. (Ephesians 5:2; 1 John 4:8)
- God is good (all the time). (Mark 10:17-18)
- God is a God of justice. (Genesis 18:25)
- God demands justice of us. (Micah 6:8)
- God is the source of wisdom. (James 1:5)
- God gives direction. (Proverbs 3:5-6; Psalm 119:105)
- God requires us to walk in purity. (1 Thessalonians 4:3)
- God rewards both good and evil. (Psalm 1:1-4)
- God is always in control (even in Disruptions). (Romans 8:28; Genesis 50:19-20)
- God is full of grace, and covers our sin. (Genesis 3:21; John 1:29; 1 John 1:9)
- God is masterful at transforming people. (Ephesians 2:1-10)

A MESS AND A MASTERPIECE

> **Ephesians 2:10 (NASB)**
> For we are [God's] workmanship, created in Christ Jesus for good works, which God prepared beforehand so that we would walk in them.

I don't know if it's OK to have a favorite verse, but I just have to say that this is my go-to verse of the Bible. I use this passage when disciplining my sons, and when congratulating them. I use it when praying over my daughters while tucking them in at night. When Karen and I get into our *intense fellowship*, I remind her that I am God's workmanship and she'd better recognize that. Maybe that last one was a bit of a stretch, but those who know me well have heard this passage come out of my mouth more than a lot! I love the verse because it is so full of promise, especially (not in spite of) knowing that life is filled with many disruptions. My past, present, and future is summed up in one verse. Both my value and my victory are in harmony with my walking and even my waiting. Momentum and maturity converge at the crossroads of this passage.

In this section, I want to use Paul's words to display a Biblical view of humanity in its truest sense. Remember the quote earlier from Stott; I would consider this to be our *freedom verse*. And if we are going to adopt his definition of freedom, *being our truest selves,* allow me to offer up an anthropology (study of mankind) based on this verse. But let me warn you, I might nerd out just a little bit. I usually keep the *theo-nerd* (theology = the study of God) tucked away until I am talking to friends from seminary, but it is beneficial here. Since the majority of the New Testament was originally written in Greek, we should look at some particular words in Greek, and take note of their significance. Let's unpack this freedom verse.

WE ARE GOD'S WORKMANSHIP (SPECIAL CREATION)

We are not God. That's all. On to the next clause. OK, maybe I should slow down and elaborate this point, because it definitely matters in times of disruption. Paul acknowledges the fact that we did not get here on our own. When we read the Bible from the very beginning, we find that Scripture states as much. We (man and woman) were created by God (Genesis 1:26-27). The Bible speaks in a unique way in this passage about our being created. Paul says that we are God's workmanship (Greek: ποίημα, poiema | that which has been made).[24] Now granted, "humankind is not alone in being the [created] object of God's love, care, and creative and sustaining power,"[25] but there is something unique about our creation. Humans are not "merely the beneficiaries of God's providential care in the way that birds and flowers are: we are active members of a fellowship of love that establishes our place as children of God and masters of creation."[26]

---

[24] ποίημα, ατος, τό, *BDAG*, 842.

[25] Anthony C. Thiselton, *Systematic Theology* (Grand Rapids, MI; Cambridge, U.K.: William B. Eerdmans Publishing Company, 2015), 114. Thiselton surveys Scripture to show that God is intimately concerned for all of his creation, including nature and the animal kingdom.

[26] Gerald Bray, *God Is Love: A Biblical and Systematic Theology* (Wheaton, IL: Crossway, 2012), 71.

First, the nerdy part; this word, poiema is only used twice in all of the *New Testament* (the books of the Bible starting with Matthew and ending with Revelation). Paul uses the word in Romans 1:20 and Ephesians 2:10. Both are only used in relation to talking about the creation of humankind. Elsewhere in the New Testament, Paul and other writers chose the word κτίσις (ktisis) which has the same meaning, but its usage is not restricted to humanity.[27] This particular word for creation is used over a dozen times, and includes everything under the sun.

Let's move from the technical argument, to the most obvious one, found in Genesis 1:26-27. God did not only create us, but we are the only part of his creation that has a blueprint. WHOA! THAT IS HUGE!!! Let's not rush past that. Since the beginning of time, mankind has been fascinated with the world around us! Science, astronomy, biology... there is no end to how far we have gone, and continue to go, in order to figure out this great world which we inhabit. But did you catch what I just said earlier?

Let me break it down. Read Genesis chapter 1, and ask yourself with each stage of creation, *'What's this supposed to look like?'* Imagine ALL that we have been able to do with light! I can sit in my living room, and watch a 4K, LIVE event on the other side of the world, simply because mankind has learned how to manipulate light. But who created the light? God did... And what was light supposed to look like? He never says. He just commanded it to exist. And this created thing, which has no blueprint, serves many purposes. We celebrate with, mourn with, cook with, operate with, we rise and slumber by, we manipulate, we capture... *light.*

But, light has no blueprint!

Being a homeschooling father, I have built a library of some of the coolest books, especially since I have boys! Some of the books that intrigue us the most are those on science and nature. A few even tell how some of our modern inventions are inspired by observing the animal kingdom, or studying nature. We have a world of blueprints to model our inventions after. But when it came to creation, only once did God stop and become an engineer; when he created you and me.

How do we know that we are a special creation? Because the first time God used a cheat sheet in his creative work was when he was creating

---

[27] κτίσις, εως, ἡ, *BDAG*, 572-73. This word includes humanity, but poiema is exclusive to humans alone.

us. And what was his blueprint? Himself! You must be really in love with yourself to create something that reflects you! God didn't simply say 'Let there be humans!' No, in fact when God created humanity, it is the first glimpse that we get into heaven, to know that God co-equally exists as a multi-person deity; he says, 'Let *us* make man in *our* image.'

When God made us, he had a conversation with himself, *Father, Spirit, and Son*. He says "Let Us make man in Our image, according to Our likeness; and let them rule over the fish of the sea and over the birds of the sky and over the cattle and over all the earth, and over every creeping thing that creeps on the earth" (Genesis 1:26, NASB). We've been made, not only with the best of blueprints, but with the most vital task of all creation. All creation (κτίσις | ktisis), humanity included was commanded to exist and some to reproduce. But humanity was the only creation (ποίημα | poiema) that would bear the very image of God, and reflect him amidst the rest of creation, "representing the love, sovereignty, care, and character of God to the world."[28]

Indeed, we are his [special] creation; but before we boast in our supremacy over the rest of creation, we must recognize what this means. To be human, the *special* creation, means that we "exercise a management role in creation on behalf of God, and are to follow the divine example of creative care."[29] To represent God means that our views and opinions of this world have to conform to his. Charles Sherlock sums up this responsibility very well:

> Our status as human beings who have dominion must be interpreted in the light of the dominion which Christ exercises; displayed in compassionate, sacrificial, costly service for the sake of others. Of primary significance in this divine service is Christ's restoration of our relationship with God (the 'upward vertical 'aspect, our 'being-with-God'; but it cannot be dissociated from the restoration of humans one with another (the 'horizontal 'aspect, our 'being-with-others'), and neither can be abstracted from

---

[28] Thiselton, *Systematic Theology*, 115.
[29] Charles Sherlock, *The Doctrine of Humanity*, ed. Gerald Bray, Contours of Christian Theology (Downers Grove, IL: InterVarsity Press, 1996), 119.

the reconciliation of all creation in and through Christ (our 'being-with-nature').[30]

What a great place to start when talking about who I am. To understand that I am created with both a model and a mission is refreshing. What that means is that disruptions aren't just inconvenient moments in my life. We will get to this a little later, but I thought it might be a good place to pause and just recognize the intentionality of God. We were made to steward that which was made.

The problem in the narrative of human history is that not too soon after we were created in a special way, the art tried to be the artist. It would be unfathomable for a fish to decide that it has no need to exist in the water, or that it would much rather try its way in the flight game; that it feels like 'flying away' (wait...is THAT what happened with penguins?!). Only humans, God's special creation, fall guilty of such ironic notions; that we know how to best live our lives. When our assessment of created order trumps the Creator's appraisal, the image is distorted. And such is what took place in the garden of Eden.

God placed a tree in the center of the garden and instructed that it not be eaten from; fruit of this tree would be of no benefit to Adam and Eve. This was God the Creator's appraisal of the tree, but not Eve's, the created. In fact, she not only assessed it as good, she saw a multi-faceted goodness in the tree. Genesis 3:6 explains that although God said to refrain, Eve felt that the tree had the ability to sustain (it was good for food), entertain (it was pleasing to the eye), and to train (it was good for wisdom). God said 'Leave it alone!' Eve said 'Lock and load!' In that moment, Eve surrendered herself to her own authority, forgetting that she is God's creation. So, the image was distorted. Hello, **DISRUPTION!**

At one point, God did break out the Holy Etch-a-Sketch on creation, and wipe the world with a flood, but the created ones (us) kept blowing it! So, instead of repeatedly erasing the canvas, God went Bob Ross on humanity. Remember Bob Ross, the white painter with the big afro and smooth voice? He would always say that there were no mistakes, only *'happy little accidents.'* Not that there is anything happy nor accidental about sin, but the point here is that Jesus was the only one who could come

---

[30] Sherlock, *The Doctrine of Humanity*, 121.

and make a masterpiece of our mess. He would cleanse us of our sin, and make us his own (Titus 2:14).

CREATED IN CHRIST JESUS

Everything said of humanity thus far is universal. You don't have to have faith in Jesus to have been made in the image of God. The image of God is the condition of every human being of every age, race, color, creed, and gender. *Red and yellow, black and white, we're created in his like(ness)* (I couldn't help it... I was feeling something there). But when Paul says that we were created *in Christ,* filters begin to be put in place. This is the point of the verse that gets a little awkward; it's that moment where things start getting good. Unfortunately, it's not going to apply to everyone. If we read further in Paul's letter to the church in Ephesus, this line of distinction becomes a little clearer.

> **Ephesians 2:11–13 (NASB)**
>
> [11] Therefore remember that formerly you, the Gentiles in the flesh, who are called "Uncircumcision" by the so-called "Circumcision," which is performed in the flesh by human hands— [12] remember that you were at that time separate from Christ, excluded from the commonwealth of Israel, and strangers to the covenants of promise, having no hope and without God in the world. [13] But now in Christ Jesus you who formerly were far off have been brought near by the blood of Christ.

Paul refers back to their most primitive existence: that they found their identity in their ethnic, social, and religious standing. Perhaps the only thing not noted here is their gender identity, but he does touch on this elsewhere in the Bible (cf. Philippians 3). Often in the New Testament, when Paul uses the phrase, *in Christ*, he is doing more than affirming his readers' belief in Jesus, the Messiah. Rather, he is reconditioning their sense of *social identity* (who I believe myself to be in a community of others). What is significant in this aim, as my friend and seminary professor, Dr. J. Brian Tucker points out, is that "Paul does not look to obliterate previous identities; rather he seeks to reprioritize them."³¹ Being in Christ doesn't mean that the realities of my ethnic, sexual, and even social identities are done away with, it means that they become reprioritized, in light of the Lordship of Christ in my life.

Although I would love to keep this point within the framework of the current text, it would be helpful to look at how Tucker has brilliantly worked with this topic in his studies on the book of 1 Corinthians. In *Remain in Your Calling*, he shows the various ways that Paul worked

> to transform the Christ-followers' Roman social identity into a hybrid, nested identity in which their Roman identity is not obliterated, but is subservient to their "in Christ" identity. This provides a social identity that would inform their ethical choices and, over time, would produce a distinct ethos in comparison with Roman imperial ideology.³²

Let me clarify his point and bring this to bear on the current discussion. As a spiritual leader, Paul is writing with an awareness of the complexities that come with simply being *created*. There are certainly *biological* complexities, as time has shown. What it means to be a man and what it means to be a woman is an issue that society still cannot seem to agree on. Only a fool would argue that there are no *ethnic* complexities. Were this true, there would be no Holocaust, no slavery, no Civil Rights movement, and no *#Blacklivesmatter*. Ethnic complexities are evidenced through the historic massacres and movements of American history. Sexual identity and race bring enough complexities to life, but "race and sex are not the only factors that shape our identity. Location, family, religious persuasion, occupation, and even personal interests play a role. Many of the factors that influence our sense of identity are beyond our control."³³ This

---

³¹ J. Brian Tucker, *Remain in Your Calling: Paul and the Continuation of Social Identities in 1 Corinthians* (Eugene, OR: Pickwick Publications, 2011), Kindle location 1267.

³² Tucker, *Remain in Your Calling*, loc. 1191. Another excellent read by Tucker, (maybe even an easier read) is his *Reading 1 Corinthians* (Eugene, OR: Wipf and Stock, 2017).

³³ J. Brian Tucker and John Koessler, *All Together Different: Upholding the Church's Unity While Honoring Our Individual Identities* (Chicago, IL: Moody Publishers, 2017), Kindle location 208.

list is in no way comprehensive; it doesn't mention our experiences, our wins and losses. It doesn't account for our political stances and our educational journey.

And in all of these things, being *in Christ* means that the Word of God tells us who we ought to be *accounting for*, not *at the neglect of* these complexities. Perhaps it is beginning to be clear why we had to start here. Imagine what this means for disruptions. Many times, a disruption might involve another person. Wait, I mean another one of God's *special creations*. We bring our identity into disruptions right along with us. Think back to our 'REAL STEEL' movie for a second, remember Jackman put on the headset so that Atom would know where to take his instructions from? Far too often, we take our instruction from various identity influencers, over and above our *in Christ* identity. At times, our ethnicity is wearing the headset, or our political views, our socioeconomic status; Jesus is our Sunday thing but not our guide in the disruption.

To be *in Christ* means that we, the special creation once marred by the effects of sin, have been redeemed by the one whose image we were created to reflect in the first place. It means that Jesus informs who Aaron j Robinson is to understand himself to be as a black, male, husband, and father, living in the inner-city. Jesus informs my decisions in the voter's box, as much as in the bedroom. I am not a Christian first, and an African American second, I am an African American Christian. In Christ does not change nor reduce my African American heritage (with a Jamaican maternal grandfather). My manhood is not diminished because I am a born-again Christian. This is how Tucker explains what Paul was writing to clarify to the early church. Christ does not change who I was created to be; rather, the Christ event in history was so that I can be the best version of me - the me that God had in mind when he created humanity in Genesis 1. To better understand this better version of me, I must ask the question, *'What am I here for?'*

FOR GOOD WORKS

Three words that make all the difference in the world. If ever there was a versatile word in the English language, it is the word 'good.' Like many other words in our daily vocabulary, it tends to hurt us when we read this word in our English Bible translations. Think about the range of meaning for *good*. At the start of their day, husband and wife greet each other, '*Good morning!*' This salutation could be a reflection of time shared the night before, or it could be an expressed desire that the day ahead would go well with them. The phrase, *'Good luck!'* is often said, but with at least two very different meanings. It could mean that one individual hopes for the other to prosper in a particular endeavor; however, it could also be a sarcastic comment, in which one individual doubts another's ability to achieve success.

There is a wide range of 'goods' that we use in our language every day, 'What's good?' 'Good grief!' 'Good call!' 'Good luck!' 'Good lovin', body rockin'...' (sorry... I say 'good' so many times, and an old R&B song is bound to pop in my head)! Whether the term is used to greet, to dismiss, to assess, or to describe the way we package food, the word 'good' falls short. In fact, given the right context, the word even means to fall short; *good* is just not enough when it comes to certain services and practices. In seminary, I didn't want to score *good* marks. I wanted to master my classes. When I ran a digital media firm, I didn't want people to say that I was good. Clients weren't looking for a good producer or editor, but a great one.

Similar to the versatility of the word 'good' is the word 'work.' Today, when we say 'work' in America, we can use that word in numerous ways. We use it adjectivally, explaining or qualifying a particular thing. 'This is a *working theory.*' Where is a *'working pen'* when you need one? We use the term verbally. We are constantly trying to *'work on ourselves.'* We *'work 9am to 5pm'* to make a living. Of course, we might rephrase that last point by saying that we have to *'go to work.'* Work takes many faces in the English language.

If both 'good' and 'work' have a broad range of meaning in our English language, then familiarity can cause some interpretive problems for us. It can cause us to read too swiftly, and move on. Let's pause for a moment and think about how our understanding of these two words can inform what we understand this passage to mean. If Scripture tells us that we were created, *in Christ*, for *good works*, what does that mean? Does this passage refer to an acceptable career? Does it refer to a holy occupation of some sort? To best understand this phrase on Paul's terms, we need to look at the Biblical definition of these words, and not our own. NERD ALERT! In the Greek, Paul says that we were created in Christ, for ἔργοις ἀγαθοῖς (ergois agathois | good works). Let's look at these words together, and come to a Biblical understanding of what it is exactly that we were created to do.

I will begin with ἔργοις (ergois | works). Paul is not speaking of a particular job or career here; and even more, he is not speaking particularly of anything that we might call 'ministry' in an organized faith-based context. Here, Paul is actually talking about regular, daily, normal tasks.[34] This definition may not be as exciting as you had hoped, but it is certainly powerful. It is both the quantity and quality of this word that makes its definition life-giving. First, it is not a singular thing that we were created to do, but a plethora of things, as noted by Paul's use of the plural. The fact that we have not been created for only one specific thing brings hope, in that it frees us of the fear that we might 'miss out'. Just as sure as #FOMO (fear of missing out) is a popular thing amongst millennials, #FOMP (fear of missing purpose) is popular amongst humans in general.

How many times have we seen stories of famous people who have achieved what most would consider the *American Dream*, yet take their lives prematurely? We later find that they struggled with depression and a never-ending search for purpose. The search for that *one particular thing* has caused so many to feel as though every *non-particular* thing does not matter. We spend our life looking for one unique task or assignment that finally gives validation to our life, but we miss the significance in all of the tasks that we carry out throughout our day. Benjamin T. Quinn and Walter R. Strickland II offer a great definition of work in this regard, suggesting that "wherever people interact with God's world—whether planting bulbs or planting churches, raising children at home or driving to the office, writing a song or writing an amicus brief—it is all work."[35]

Don't read past that definition too swiftly. This definition means that not only is Paul not talking about a *singular* act or task, but he is not talking about a *sacred* (related to the church) versus a *secular* (related to the world) work either. It is not uncommon to read such a meaning into this verse; as if Paul is saying that God only created us to do things in and for the local church – all other tasks are secondary. It is critically important to understand that "a worldview divided into sacred and secular spheres undermines the

---

[34] ἔργον, ου, τό, *BDAG*, 390-91.
[35] Benjamin T. Quinn and Walter R. Strickland II, *Every Waking Hour: An Introduction to Work and Vocation for Christians* (Bellingham, WA: Lexham Press; Southeastern Baptist Theological Seminary, 2016), 7.

teachings of Scripture (Gen 1:1; 1 Tim 4:4) and fails to recognize that the Christian life as a whole is dedicated to the Lord."[36]

Allow me to share a final word on the nature of our work, before we discuss the value of our work. We should not misunderstand this to be a 'career' word. Granted, there is much to be said about how our careers can be used to glorify God. I enjoy reading articles and devotions on this topic. I firmly believe that "work can create ways to help people thrive; it can discover the depths of God's creation; and it can bring us into wonderful relationships with co-workers and those who benefit from our work (customers, clients, patients, and so forth)."[37] God does amazing things through professionals who live out their faith in the marketplace, but this passage is not referring to a career or occupation. The definition of the word bears repeating; ἔργοις (ergois | works) means everything that we do. So just what is special about this work? Well, it's *good*!

The Greek word that Paul uses here for *good* is ἀγαθοῖς (agathois). The range of meaning for this word is not as broad and interchangeable as our English *good*.[38] When it pertains to activity, the word means actions that meet a high standard of worth and merit.[39] This word is not just a matter of assessment, but we should think of it in the sense of social engagement; something that is beneficial to another.[40] So then, one of the major identity markers of those who are *in Christ*, is that our lives are lived out in some fashion to benefit others. Who we are does not change, but the benefactors of what we do indeed changes (see what I just did there? *in deed... in work...* Thanks folks, I'll be here all night!).

What is profound about this word good reaches back to Old Testament Jewish thought. While we might be satisfied to evaluate the word good on our own terms, such was not the case for the Jewish community.

---

[36] Quinn and Strickland, *Every Waking Hour*, 10.

[37] William Messenger, "Introduction to the Theology of Work," in *Genesis through Revelation*, ed. William Messenger, vol. 1, Theology of Work Bible Commentary (Peabody, MA: Hendrickson Publishers, 2014–2016), 1.

[38] Although Moisés Silva, ἀγαθός, *NIDNTTE*, 93, suggests that the word had a similar semantic range as the English word 'good,' I would argue that the assessment discounts urban vernacular (slang), especially that of the 21st Century, and millennial interaction... I mean, 'drippin' now refers to dressing sharply!

[39] ἀγαθός, ή, όν, *BDAG*, 3-4.

[40] ἀγαθός, ή, όν, *Louw and Nida*, 741.

The word ἀγαθός (agathos) was deeply connected to the Jewish concept of God; in fact, for the Jews it was unfathomable for anything good to exist apart from God.[41] A New Testament example of this can be seen in Jesus' response when he is called *'good teacher'* (see Luke 18:19 and Mark 10:18). Jesus' response makes perfect sense when we have a better understanding of the word; he asks, *'Why do you call me good? No one is good except God alone!'* Even when good was seen in people, it would ultimately be understood to be a reflection of an intimate relationship with God.

We see a connection running full circle here. God creates us for activity that should reflect to the world our intimate relationship with him. The relationship between *good* and *works* has explosive potential. In a world that is hostile to God, Jesus teaches that our 'good works' should turn the attention of the world from us toward God.

> **Matthew 5:16 (NASB)**
> Let your light shine before men in such a way that they may see your *good works*, and glorify your Father who is in heaven.

Ultimately, this phrase *'We are God's workmanship, created in Christ Jesus, for good works...'* could safely be translated, 'God redeemed his broken creation, through Jesus Christ, for a purpose!' What a closer look at a Biblical definition of 'good works' helps us to see is that purpose is not a singular lane, it's a fiber optic cable network - all working together, to point the rest of God's creation back to the Creator. That is our purpose – to allow the love and grace that we have experienced through Christ to shine in everything that we do. This purpose extends to every person who is *in Christ*; the corporate executive, the blue-collar worker, the teacher, the lawyer, the medical professional, the pastor, the missionary, the actor and actress... AND... the father, the mother, the sibling, the student. This purpose is for every believer in every place, every gender, age, and race!

MY OWN EVOLUTION OF GOOD WORKS

At the age of sixteen, I felt the strong desire to enter the ministry. Our Pastor, Tim Dilena, had a way of making Scripture palatable. Under his preaching and teaching, I witnessed a dramatic change in the circumstances

---

[41] Moisés Silva, ἀγαθός, *NIDNTTE*, 93-94.

of my household. This is what I wanted to do with the rest of my life; make the Word of God come alive in the hearts of others. As I grew older, I began to serve in various positions within the church. I served as an intern, a worship leader, children and youth ministry leader, and more. A couple years after graduating high school, I proposed to Karen, and we were married a year later. The serving roles in the church continued; young adult director, youth pastor, media pastor, and associate pastor.

Still feeling 'called' (a Christian term, simply meaning *created for this*) to ministry, I had to take work outside of the church, in order to support my growing family. For years, I worked in various jobs: banking specialist, hardware engineer, job training director. I hated my jobs. I thought that they were **DISRUPTIONS**. This mindset came in part from growing up in a home with a hard-working father, who seemed to dread going to work. It excited him to do anything for the church, but when it came time to go to General Motors, he referred to it as going to the *'plantation'*. It was not because the work conditions for over thirty years were reminiscent of slavery, but that he simply saw no value in the work he did there. That was especially true compared to work at the church, whether that be preaching, carpentry, ushering, or lawn care.

As much as I was reading the Word, a lot of tradition and personal experiences informed how I understood what I was reading. When I would read words like 'work,' I surely thought that the Bible was talking about work in the church. Why would God create us for anything other than that? I thought that working for the church, or any job specifically tasked with the proclamation of the gospel, was the pinnacle of work. One day, while working as a job training director, I felt like my life was void of purpose. Although I was working for a Christian organization, it was not the local church. I was not leading devotionals, spiritual retreats, or teaching Bible lessons. We prayed when we met, but only as an opener to start the day's work. My job was teaching teenagers how to apply for a job, prepare a resume, and build the soft skills necessary for job retention. This wasn't the kind of work that I was *called* to do (there is that word again).

So, I tendered my resignation and told my executive director that I felt God calling me to pursue my purpose – 'real ministry.' I was young, uninformed, and passionate about the local church, but she was graceful, and prayed with me as she accepted my resignation. I gave a little over a month's notice, then I left to start a digital media business so that I could have a more flexible schedule and help co-lead our youth group.

We had yet another problem. My family grew. The business grew. Over the years, I found myself hating my business. This was not what I was called to do – this was not my purpose. Even when I would receive rave reviews on the work that I did, I would be sure to let people know that this business was temporary – I was called to ministry. As you are reading this, you might imagine the many **DISRUPTIONS** that this mindset created. I would constantly complain about the work that I was doing. I liked making money, but I hated not being at the church all of the time. I envied my friends who were working for the local church. While I was on video shoots, or late-night edits, they were prepping for camps and retreats. They were meeting students at the flagpoles for prayer. "This is not fair! I hate this!" My household began to suffer under the weight of a husband and father who misunderstood what a Biblical view of work (and calling) was. The more my family grew, the more my family needed. The more my family needed, the more that I needed to work. **DISRUPTIONS!** At least that's what I thought, until God gave me exactly what I asked for!

An opportunity came up for me to serve as the youth pastor (something I have always been passionate about) at the church where I was serving. I walked away from my business, and gave myself *fully* to that work! Did you hear that?! I was finally doing the Lord's *work!* Ephesians 2:10 had finally become a reality for me! That was the mindset that I had anyway. I put more heart and effort into this new career than any job that I had ever served in before. And the youth ministry grew! But a problem arose: the economy began to suffer and as a result, so was the small inner-city church where I was serving on staff. Everyone had been affected by these troubled times. It was a season where people were trying to refinance their mortgages for lower rates, or worse, walking away from mortgages over their heads. Many were trying to downsize their sport utility vehicles for more fuel-efficient cars. Unfortunately for me, I had two mortgages (a home, and a two-family rental), and drove a Ford Expedition with a Triton V-8 engine and all the bells and whistles… **DISRUPTION** on several levels!

Eventually it took conversations with a man who had befriended me, and is today one of my dearest friends and a fatherly mentor, Larry Johnson, to help me see how flawed my thinking was. They were not scholarly conversations. There was no reference of Greek words or systematic theology terms. It was just a testimony of a man who knew that he was called to do the work of the Lord. But that work was primarily taking care of his greatest ministry, his family. This dialogue was affirmed by my executive pastor at that time. Pastor Kevin had served nearly all of his adult years in ministry. He was about four years older than me, was married a few years longer, and had children around the same age as mine. There were enough similarities about his life that he could teach me some lessons on serving God *in all* areas of my life, *with all* areas of my life, and not just when I'm working for the church.

Although Kevin had worked for the church before, there were times that he served in churches that did not have the budget to hire a full-time pastor and support his family. So, Kevin started his own company. He successfully ran a business that not only supported him in working for the local church, but through this business venture, he also supported other ministries. He sponsored missionaries, funded outreach efforts, and gave generously to people in need. Having sold his successful company years back, Larry was not only financially supporting the work of the Lord, but he and his wife Marilyn had now given themselves full-time to ministry in the inner-city while still mentoring business-minded individuals.

Through many conversations, Larry and Kevin began to help me break down the wall that I had built in error between sacred and secular work. They helped me to better understand that "it is a mistake to think that the Christian worldview is operating only when we are doing such overtly Christian activities [like working for the church]." [42] Instead, my faith in God should be a lens through which I viewed everything in the world, including work. Ultimately, they helped me see that I would not be disappointing God, but rather honoring God if I stepped away from a struggling paid position at the local church and resumed something that I was quite good at, multimedia production. It was very clear that they were helping me see the unnecessary disruptions that I was causing in my household, because I had a faulty view of work.

This faulty view also caused marital stress and financial battles. We were not able to enjoy things like a regular date night, a family vacation, or small family escapes from the hectic life of urban ministry. All of these *healthy* things were missing because I could not see that God had given me the ability to create wealth. I ignored that work for what I thought to be the more important work. Larry began to mentor me in what it meant to be an entrepreneur who glorified God with his work and his wealth. Having

---

[42] Timothy Keller and Katherine Leary Alsdorf, *Every Good Endeavor: Connecting Your Work to God's Work* (New York: Dutton, 2012), 179–180.

children my age and older, Larry would offer advice to me as a father would a son – even at times calling me out for my unhealthy balance of 'church work' and family. He would remind me what my primary ministry ought to be. I remember when I finally walked into the church office and handed Pastor Tim my letter of resignation. It was a tearful walk into the office. *What would he think of me? I am not spiritual! I am not a man of faith! I am not called!* Quite the opposite! He too began to teach me *a more excellent way*. I will not forget the words he said to me that day:

> Aaron, I would not be any less proud to say that I have a spiritual son who is a loving husband, father, and creative media producer, than I would to say that I have spiritual son who works for me as a youth pastor. What makes me most proud, and more than that, brings God pleasure, is that you faithfully serve him, and steward your family. This is your calling!

So I stopped working at the church and resumed my business, but this time with a different mindset – much different. When my mind changed about my work, everything changed! I looked at new contracts as new assignments from God! Many doors for the gospel were open, through weddings, executive meetings, and creative brainstorming sessions. More so, I was able to share (or simply reflect) the gospel of Jesus Christ in ways and places that I would never have been able to from my position in the local church. I am not suggesting that I had lost the desire to serve there, simply that I had learned to appreciate where God had me at the time, trusting that if and when he would have need of me in the local church, he would make provision for it. There was one problem. While I had a Biblical view of my occupation, I was still missing the non-paid work in which I was to glorify God. I wasn't just a producer. I was also a partner to my wife and a parent to my kids.

I was so focused on being a provider that I forgot the rest of the instructions from the other conversations with these men of God. Besides my being a good financial provider, what was the 'highly esteemed benefit' (good) of all of my at-home activities (works) for my wife and children? All of my focus of 'good works' were external to the most important place – *home*! Unfortunately, this realization would not come until years later after many, many **DISRUPTIONS!** It wasn't until my first semester at Moody Theological Seminary that the light came on! In my Introduction to Theological Research class, the topic that we had to research was…you guessed it…WORK! Now, more than pastoral counseling, great mentoring, and entrepreneurial coaching, I would have to read scholars and theologians who have wrestled with this topic for decades…even centuries. This study led me back to a passage that I had loved for so long, *Ephesians 2:10*, and this new 'Theology of Work' radically transformed my private life: my marriage, my parenting, and personal stewardship.[43] Work, good work, was every single thing that I had a responsibility to do. Biblically speaking, even my leisure and recreation fall under this category. I have an opportunity, at every turn, to honor God.

WHICH GOD PREPARED BEFOREHAND

It was late October, and love was in the air; however, only a few dollars were in my pocket. There was no way that I was going to sit idly and let the rest of the world enjoy this romantic day, and not get in on the action. I mean, let's be clear, this would be the second time in my life that I would actually be able to enjoy this day in a relationship! It was Sweetest Day, and Karen and I had been dating just a little over a year. The year prior, we probably went to Taco Bell, and a movie. I really don't remember. This time, we'd been dating for a year. Karen was my first girlfriend, so it's not like I had a lot of practice with this, but having been dating for over a year, I was not going to drop the ball. Until I dropped the ball.

Although I had never as much as boiled an egg for Karen, I decided that instead of her favorite restaurant, I would have her over for a romantic, candle-lit dinner. I even got sparkling grape juice to make the night extra special! When asked why I didn't think about renting a movie, I gave Karen the most sensible answer. I thought we'd talk the night away at the table, with a lot of slow-motion laughs like they do in the movies. Yeah, that didn't go over well. I guess it is because I attempted to cook the most elaborate meal, and let's just say a couple sliders and some potato chips would have been an upgrade. I didn't even get the grape juice in the fridge fast enough for it to chill. It was all a disaster. So, I did what any man seeking to save the night would do. I picked up her younger sister and my best friend, who were also good friends, and suggested we just go for a nice ride. '*Where, Aaron!? We live in Detroit!*' Well, I lived five minutes from the bridge to

---

[43] This is the Cliff's Notes version of my testimony, but Karen and I are working on a marriage and family project that pulls back the curtain a bit more to share some of our journey to stewardship of our lives.

Canada, and hey, I *did* have a few dollars in my pocket. I had a full tank of gas and enough for the toll over the bridge.

Karen was upset and embarrassed! Not only was I ruining a romantic day and blowing a date night, now I am bringing witnesses along and driving aimlessly out of the country. I mean, first girlfriend is one thing, but there are some things I should have just known…I guess. The entire time, I could just feel her thoughts… 'This joker says he loves me, and this is his best expression of love? He couldn't even put in the effort to save up for a good date night…*on Sweetest Day*!' Fair enough, but at least I was trying! I drove her down some of the most beautiful streets of Windsor. She even admitted that the scenery was beautiful. We drove through nice neighborhoods, just admiring big houses (it's a thing we liked to do…who am I kidding…still do!). We rolled past cool structures and through small towns where other couples were out on dates. Karen was getting hungry, and I had ruined dinner. I only had enough money to get back home, so I reluctantly allowed her to spring for dinner at a local fast-food spot. It was either that or risk her getting vocally frustrated!

As we began our journey back to the states, I could tell that I had blown it! There was no salvaging this night. Not even Ben Tankard, my favorite Christian Jazz artist at the time could help. Then I saw something that I thought would *surely* bring me back into saving graces. As we passed a park, I saw a lady with a horse and carriage. The carriage was beautiful, and there was not a soul in sight. I looked at Karen with a familiar look. If brown could turn red, that is precisely what happened to her face. I am known to joke with cashiers and ask them if they can just let me have something for free – it makes them laugh, and leads to the funniest conversations. I looked at Karen and pleaded with her – 'let's just give it a try!' I mean, the place looked dead, and the lady looked nice. Would she let this young couple get just a ten-minute ride? I think Karen only got out of the car so that this embarrassing 'no' that I would hear would give her the ammunition she needed to break up with me. Never had I seen her walk with such anger.

As we approached the carriage I simply asked, '*Excuse me, ma'am. How much is a ride on your carriage?*' Embarrassed by the very thought of me asking, Karen reminded me (not subtly whatsoever) that I had no money. Before I could respond to Karen, the lady graciously did for me. '*That's OK, sweetheart… It's Sweetest Day, and I don't have anyone else lining up for a ride right now…why don't the four of you hop on in, and I'll take you around the park!'* Well, she might have been embarrassed, but God's favor was with us that night. Karen was mad, but she (and her sister and my friend) proceeded toward the carriage. Being the gentleman that I am, I took her hand and helped her into the carriage – help which she refused. She was mad! I could tell. Everyone could tell.

When Karen sat down mad, embarrassed, feeling unloved, undervalued, almost fighting tears of disgust, she glanced at the seat in front of her. There was an over-sized card with her name on it and a dozen long-stemmed roses. At the realization that I had thought through the evening quite thoroughly, we both began to get teary-eyed. She wrapped her arms around me and settled in for a nice cuddly ride around the park on this brisk fall evening. The driver took us around the park showing us scenes that were far more beautiful than the car ride. She even took us by a gorgeous fountain in the center of the park and *demanded* that we get out and get a picture by it – all couples do, she informed us. So, we did, even though we're not much of the fountain type.

As we walked along the fountain, Karen held my hand and just let out a sigh that let me know she was pleased with me. As we stood still, I'll never forget the song that we heard in the distance, 'You Are So Beautiful to Me.' I took her in my arms and just began to sing to this instrumental melody that kept drawing closer and closer. Suddenly, Karen looked up as the man with the radio got uncomfortably close, sat his boombox near us, and walked away. *'Aaron! Was that Kala!?'* Yes, it was my older brother Kala. *'Is that your parents?'* Yes, it was. And before she could even call out the other of our loved ones who were scattered in the park that night, she looked up and found me on one knee, holding the biggest investment I had ever made in my life. What seemed to be the worst date in her life was a masterful plan for her to step into the journey of a lifetime as my wife.

You see, much better than a Greek lesson here, or the history of Old Testament or New, I wanted to paint a very real picture of what it means that God has *prepared beforehand* the works that we are supposed to walk in. OK, maybe one point from the Greek: the word προετοιμάζω (proetoimazō | prepared beforehand) is *only* used to describe work that God has done.[44] Let me state it better this way. I'm sure that as some were reading this, you may have been predicting the ending of the story. At the end, you could say,

---

[44] Προετοιμάζω, *BDAG,* 869.

'Good job, Aaron!' But all my behind-the-scenes work was limited by so much; time, experience, finances. If a finite man such as I can work such a masterful plan, with all my limitations, can you imagine the work that God does behind the scenes to make sure that you and I end up in the place where we need to be? All Karen had to do to change the trajectory of her life was get in the car, get in the carriage, and ultimately say 'Yes!' in spite of the roller coaster of emotions that she may have been going through.

While we might understand this point, the final question is *before what?* Of this, we need no long explanation. We have already determined that it is *God* who has done the prep work, so it is safe to say, *before this!* As you read through the story above, it didn't matter when I purchased the ring. It didn't matter how long ago I had the band from our church record the instrumental song. Whether I reserved the horse and carriage a month prior or the week prior didn't matter. These were all great points to tell Karen later, as she was trying to see how cleverly I had pulled this off, but none of these factors had anything to do with her 'Yes!' God prepared you and me for the work that he created us for, before we were even assigned to it. *If it's yours to do, it was made for you!*

SO THAT WE WOULD WALK IN THEM

I know that it might feel like you leaped into an introductory course to Biblical languages, but there is one more important phrase that we ought to look at, before we conclude this chapter. Paul says that God went ahead of us and prepared these works, ἵνα ἐν αὐτοῖς περιπατήσωμεν (hina en autois peripatēsōmen). Of this phrase, two words are especially important, ἵνα (hina | so that) and περιπατήσωμεν (peripatēsōmen | would walk). First, we must acknowledge the powerful conjunction. As this verse relates to purposes, Paul is making it clear that the preparatory work that God has done will lead to absolute results. [45] To be clear, this is no 'left foot – right foot' statement; the phrase is not talking about the literal act of walking. Even while the term is meant figuratively, the figurative example is still

---

[45] Daniel B. Wallace, *Greek Grammar beyond the Basics: An Exegetical Syntax of the New Testament* (Grand Rapids, MI: Zondervan, 1996), 473, notes that "what God purposes is what happens and, consequently, ἵνα is used to express both the divine purpose and the result

significant: the walking is not a straight line, but rather a roaming about.⁴⁶ Therefore in a figurative sense, the word speaks to the ambiguous nature of how fulfilling one's purpose is; it is not linear, but rather a fluid manner of doing that which God has intended. The word also means, as you may have guessed, a person's habits or life conduct.

Simply put, God has gone before us and prepared situations and scenarios throughout our life that organically lead to the fulfillment of our very reason for existing. The *in Christ* factor of the equation cannot be missed. The ἵνα (hina | so that) conjunction brings it all together. The reason that Christ gave his life was not merely to make heaven a possibility (John 3:16); much more, it was so that we might experience, here on earth, that which he has declared in heaven (Matthew 6:10). At the same time, our purpose is made possible only by the work of Christ. It is for this reason that men and women can achieve financial wealth, prosperity, fame, and notoriety without Christ, yet never feel as though they accomplished anything in life – it is because it is in Jesus that we live, move and find our reason for being (Acts 17:28).

THE OLD TWENTY DOLLAR BILL BIT...

When Karen and I served as youth pastors, I preached a sermon series entitled **'Unmasked: We Are His Superheroes!'** The whole series was based on Ephesians 2:10. I compared God to Stan Lee, and humanity to all of the Marvel heroes. I told them that just as Stan Lee had sat down and crafted a storyline for Spiderman, Ironman, and all those other characters, God has a storyline laid out for us. Good thing the kids didn't see the flaw in my preaching. Spiderman, Antman, and the Black Panther cannot decide suddenly that they no longer want to follow the script. They save who Stan Lee says to save. They jump when he says jump, and they fall in love with whomever has been written into their script. This is not the case with us. While you and I may have been made in the image and likeness of God, we oftentimes abandon his will for ours – his desires for our convenience and comfort. We sometimes abandon our superhero script for a villain role not written for us.

---

⁴⁶ Περιπατέω, *BDAG*, 803, defines the walking, "to go here and there in walking, go about, walk around."

As we turn our attention toward bringing definition to disruptions, perhaps it might be helpful to speak briefly to those readers who might be a little discouraged because their life is far from aligned with God's purpose. Perhaps you are reading and you feel like this is all good information, but three years, one decision, or one broken marriage too late. Let me encourage you with an illustration that I remember from my youth pastoring days. A preacher stood in front of the congregation and held up a twenty-dollar bill. 'Is there anyone who would like this twenty-dollar bill?' he asked. Obviously, every hand in the room went up! He invited a young man to come up, and asked him what he would do with the money. The young man answered by naming some of his favorite foods, candies, and even what he'd put up for later. As he reached out his hand, the preacher snatched the twenty-dollar bill back and crumpled it up. He asked the young man if he'd still want the money. 'Of course!' exclaimed the young man. The preacher looked perplexed. 'Why would you want this money even though I balled it up?' he asked. 'Because! I can *still* spend it!' the young boy answered. The preacher then took the wadded-up bill, threw it on the floor, and jumped up and down on it! Surely the young man wouldn't want it *now*! But the young man insisted... it's *still* a twenty-dollar bill!

What the young man recognized about that money, we often fail to realize about ourselves: God created us with value and a purpose. Although we may have been crumpled by the effects of sin, stomped on by the evils of this world, and altogether mauled by the various entanglements that our own selfishness and greed have caused, it does not change what God desires to and is able to do in and through our lives. Friend, regardless of what you have experienced in your life, regardless of the disruptions you may have encountered or are facing right now, be encouraged in this:

YOU ARE GOD'S WORKMANSHIP,

CREATED IN CHRIST JESUS,

FOR GOOD WORKS,

WHICH GOD PREPARED BEFOREHAND,

SO THAT YOU WOULD WALK IN THEM.

QUESTIONS FOR REFLECTION

1. In this chapter, I argue that we need to draw a line of demarcation; that we need to clearly understand who God is and we are. Would you agree that this is a necessary starting point? *Explain why or why not.*

2. What do you find most challenging about having a Biblical understanding of who God is?

3. How can a wrong view of God create a disruption in your life?

4. What are some of the wrong views of God that you have previously held?

5. Can you identify the influence(s) on your views of God?

6. The Bible says that we are the *workmanship* of God. Oftentimes, we feel like the twenty-dollar bill that I described. What do you find most challenging about having a Biblical understanding of who God says that you are?

7. In this chapter, I have listed a non-comprehensive list of Bible verses that help to anchor our understanding of who God is, according to his Word. What passages might you add to this list?

8. What passages, other than Ephesians 2:10, can you list that help anchor our understanding of who you are (our value and our purpose), according to God's Word?

2 DEFINITION: WHAT IS GOING ON?

It is almost comical how subjective our world has become. There seem to be almost no clear boundaries. Sadly, this is true for nearly everything from sexual identity to the way we solve math problems, to the way we interpret Scripture. I heard it said once that he who defines terms controls the conversation; perhaps it might be wise for us to decide what we mean when we say disruption. In this chapter, I aim to establish a definition for the term, then peel back the curtain and discuss some 'behind the scenes' issues.

AN INTERRUPTION OR DISRUPTION?

Interruptions take place in our lives all of the time. They are not negative by nature. In fact, some interruptions are not only welcomed, but sought after. According to *Webster's Dictionary*, to interrupt is simply a matter of breaking continuity or stopping the continuous process of something. Some things we want interrupted: monotony, boredom, illness, negative generational patterns, negative statistics. In the business world, *'to interrupt'* is to take the industry by surprise with creativity, innovation, or performance. Think of a star athlete coming into the NBA and breaking records that have been championed for decades. That player *interrupted* the game! While we may not often use the term in a positive manner, we cannot argue against the fact that interruptions come in many different fashions.

It is when the interruption is a problem for us that we encounter a disruption. A disruption is when *a disturbance or a problem* breaks continuity or stops a process. We will discuss later how good can come out of a disruption – that is the whole idea behind the writing of this book; but, what we cannot sweep too swiftly over is the fact that disruptions are problematic moments or events in our lives that bring progress to a screeching halt. Even more, what is celebratory for some, can be trouble for others. Pregnancy, for example, can be a celebrated interruption for a married couple who have been planning, and perhaps even praying for children. But for someone who is the victim of rape, what should be a beautiful interruption in life becomes a horrific **DISRUPTION**! The same follows for death. There are some cases where death is a bitter-sweet interruption; saddened by loss, but at peace, regarding the end of suffering. However, losing a loved one who was the innocent victim of a senseless, violent crime or negligence, can certainly be a **_DISRUPTION_** for the family. Life, death, and many things in between can be disruptions.

Just as sure as the scenarios differ, so do the levels of severity when it comes to disruptions. A flat tire for one person could mean that they have to take the second car to work, or call for an Uber to get to their destination; yet, for another person, that flat tire could cost them their very job as they do not have the means or resources to commute any other way – they barely had enough money to fill the tank. A temporary loss of electricity can cause some families to enjoy some family time, *unplugged*. For another family, it could be the detriment of an entrepreneur whose business depends on her working on the computer, interacting with clients via the web. The scenarios and the severity make defining disruptions incredibly complex, but still, define we must, or risk missing valuable lessons.

Taking our previous discussion about ourselves into account – being made image bearers of God, redeemed in Christ, to engage in activities and events (prepared beforehand) that benefit both our immediate and broader communities, how should we best define disruptions? Allow me to set a definition that speaks to our person (the workmanship of God), our purpose (to do good works), and God's plan (which have been prepared beforehand). Such a definition would help us to recognize events in our lives more clearly for what they are; to be able to distinguish between an irritation, an interruption, and a disruption.

> A disruption is any hardship (event, action, word, or thought) which has the effect of temporarily or permanently distorting the workmanship (person), disconnecting the relationship (created in Christ), dismantling the craftsmanship (to do *good* works), denying the authorship (*God* prepared beforehand), and defying leadership (that we *should* walk in them) that our life ought to reflect.

That is a lot more than what Webster offers, but think about this definition and the moments in your life that would be categorized by one or more of these criteria. Before we advance further with discussions about hypothetical disruptions, let's look further at this definition. Notice how multi-faceted a disruption can be? It is the one storm that you cannot prepare for…or at least one you weren't prepared for. In fact, I find it ironic that in times of disruption, private or corporate, there always exists a person or group of people who can point out what could have and should have been done to avoid the disruption; whether it is what someone could have done to prevent their marriage from suffering, or what the government could have done to prevent 9/11 or COVID-19. After all the dust settles the reality is, the disruption was not avoided, and now people must navigate through the effects.

HARDSHIPS

A disruption is first and foremost a hardship that comes in the form of an event, action, word, or thought. We readily understand events and actions, but we should be sure not to underestimate the power of words spoken. James chapter 3 reminds us of how true this is. Of all things we have learned to master, the tongue is something that we have not been able to control. Crazy, right? We have put people on the moon, and taught monkeys to ask for dinner, but have not figured out how to be consistent in the way we talk to people. Proverbs 18:21 suggests that our words can bring life *and* death. The words that we hear can be disruptions in our life. In fact, I would suggest that we consider how many disruptive actions and events began with thoughts and words.

The atrocities of history will find their genesis in the mind. Imagine some of the greatest disruptions of our world's history – dig deep. Think beyond COVID-19. Begin with the scene in the Garden of Eden: a conversation with the serpent, and a divergent thought about the fruit of the forbidden tree gave birth to an action which sparked an event... **HUMANITY DISRUPTED!** How do Bible-believing explorers take people of other colors as chattel, instead of navigational partners, give them derogatory names and labels, strip them of their heritage, language, and identity, and enslave them for centuries? How does an intelligent, Bible-reading, young, charismatic German leader rise to power and give rise to one of the most horrific events in history?

Even today, in the era of #BlackLivesMatter, we are still witnessing horrific events unfolding in the news that have nothing to do with a virus. As I write this chapter, people all over the nation have risen to voice their outrage at the shooting of Ahmad Aubrey, a 25-year-old unarmed African American who was fatally shot by a Caucasian man while jogging through his own neighborhood. Centuries have passed, but the mind of humanity is still under the effects of sin. *Thoughts* still give birth to *words*, which ultimately inform *actions* that engineer *events*. Before Paul affirmed the Ephesians in 2:10, he reminded them of who they *were*:

> **Ephesians 2:1–3 (NASB)**
>
> ¹ And you were dead in your trespasses and sins, ² in which you formerly walked according to the course of this world, according to the prince of the power of the air, of the spirit that is now working in the sons of disobedience. ³ Among them we too all formerly lived in the lusts of our flesh, indulging the desires of the flesh and of the mind, and were by nature children of wrath, even as the rest.

Consider the insightful words of Dr. Mark Jobes, president of Moody Bible College, on how powerful thoughts are:

> Distorted thinking is like a bad recording that plays over and over in our heads convincing us of a false reality. Eventually that distorted message shapes and defines the way we see our world. Those messages in our head repeat lies about our identity and destiny. Distorted thinking inevitably drives us to missteps that only perpetuate our state of being stuck. Like insects trapped in the sticky web of a hungry spider, the more we struggle to escape, the more entangled we become.[47]

Thoughts, words, actions, and activities; at any stage, these can present **DISRUPTIONS**! Whether it is on a global level like genocide and slavery, domestic level like verbal or physical abuse, or somewhere in between like economic crashes, failed attempts at opportunities, addictions, loss of loved ones, or neglect, we have all felt the effects of a real **DISRUPTION**, as defined earlier. How do we know that we have felt the effects? Because the hardship we faced (thought, word, action, or event) had a direct adverse impact on your embodiment of Ephesians 2:10.

---

[47] Mark Jobes, *UNSTUCK: Out of Your Cave, Into Your Call* (Chicago, IL: Moody, 2014), 38.

DISTORTING THE WORKMANSHIP

Sometimes the hardships that we face lead us to legitimate identity crises. Tucker and Koessler are spot on when they suggest that our society as a whole is suffering through the effects of an identity crisis, and that its disorienting effects are clearly seen![48] While we have already argued that we were created in the image of God, some of us face hardships that lead us to believe that God made a mistake. Jerry Bridges explores this issue of identity crisis, and explains that when we are wrestling with the way God made us, it is ultimately an example of how "our sinful nature distorts that which God has made."[49] Some have faced mental or emotional (thought) hardships that led to a distortion of the workmanship. Where it was once taboo to even think about changing the biological distinctions (gender, race) with which we were created, it is now celebrated, championed, and brought center stage for our entertainment.[50] Whether it be a biological transformation, self-mutilation, addiction, or inability to rightly steward our body, disruptions come and distort the image of God in which we were created.

DISCONNECTING THE RELATIONSHIP

Not all hardships cause an identity crisis; at least not directly. Some lead to a spiritual disconnection. One of my favorite stories in the Bible is the story of Zacchaeus. You can correctly call him a crooked tax collector. Join with the crowd, if you may, to shout chants of 'this man is a sinner!' But, according to Matthew 19, it was not his crookedness or shady tax dealings that separated him from Jesus. It was his height! He was short and there was a crowd. His story taught me a valuable lesson: some people have a legitimate reason why they have not put their faith in Jesus! I can only imagine how difficult it may be for some to place faith and trust in a savior whose human representatives have so poorly introduced him. Unfortunately, pastors, preachers, and Christians in general are human, and some of us have misrepresented Jesus, be it through our actions (or inaction), our words (or silence), or poor stewardship of our positions as the arms and feet of Jesus.

---

[48] Tucker and Koessler, *Altogether Different*, 16.

[49] Jerry Bridges, *Trusting God* (Colorado Springs, CO: NavPress, 1988), 162.

[50] Consider the hot stories of celebrities and leaders, such as Bruce Jenner who made the public transformation to Caitlin Jenner, or Rachel Dolezal, a Caucasian who identified as African American. For entertainment consider RuPaul's VH-1 hit show, 'Drag Race.'

It is not just the misrepresentation of Jesus by people who claim to be his followers that has caused disruptions. Many people have not given Christianity a chance because of an event in their life that caused them to look at alternative options for living. Tragedies happen without answer. Loved ones are lost. Innocent people suffer. We witness large-scale violence and senseless acts. Even natural disasters that have caused loss have understandably caused some to 'shake their fists at heaven' in anger toward God. This anger creates a chasm between the Creator and his creation – a disconnect in the relationship that he desires and has designed us to have with him. This is one of the effects of disruptions.

DISMANTLING THE CRAFTMANSHIP

The disruptions that dismantle are some of the most dangerous ones. These are the sorts of disruptions that lead to isolation (we do everything alone), procrastination (we put off doing), or fossilization (we don't do, we remain). Remember we were created in Christ *to do good works*, and we discussed that 'good' is a word with social implications. That being the case, it would make sense that isolation is "an emotionally lethal condition…" and one of the most dangerous places to find ourselves in the midst of a disruption.[51] Sometimes, we face disruptions that cause us to no longer trust people, thus the 'work' we do is done not only *by* ourselves, but *for* ourselves.

Maybe it has not caused us to give up on people, but it has caused us to point out every single excuse as to why we aren't making progress. Perhaps it is the disruption of the loss of a job that now causes you to buy into the idea that you are un-hirable, or that there is a system that is stacked against you, preventing you to advance in a career. I dare not make the argument that we live in a society of completely balanced systems; my point is that we find ourselves unable to progress for the observation and commentary about those unjust systems. We don't admit to giving up in our mind, we are still 'about that work!' but when we step back and look at ourselves, we are drowning in a sea of procrastination. We're looking for someone or something to blame. It is almost as if we have made the disruption our point of destination; instead of navigating through it, we have made ourselves at home there!

---

[51] Jobes, *UNSTUCK*, 37.

Finally, disruptions can stop the work altogether. Oftentimes, these occurrences are extremely personal, such as a failure. Some have faced a disruption that has literally caused them to throw up their hands and say, 'I can go no further!' Those individuals are taken captive by their past failures and mistakes, and they lack the mental and emotional strength to carry the baggage of regret.[52] John Maxwell says that when we live in regret, we are ultimately incapable to live in ultimate freedom; that is, we are unable to do 'good works,' the very thing that we were created for. Disruptions can be events that stop us dead in our tracks.

You may wonder why I consider 'dismantling' disruptions those of the most dangerous types. The reason is that it is easy to 'live through' these disruptions. Divorce, burnt out leaders offering resignations, public moral failures, bankruptcy; none of these things are results of an overnight event. These are the effects of an individual (or individuals) who experienced a disruption, and no one knew, until it was too late. They kept working, but their motive for working shifted inward; it was no longer for the benefit of others, it was just to survive. Or they kept working, having all the appearance of engagement, but fostering a cynical outlook toward all involved, be it a ministry, a marriage, a job, a project, or whatever they were committed to. Or they just show no sign of life or vision, and instead of withdrawing, they are dismissed from their role – and others suffer because of it.

DENYING THE AUTHORSHIP

It may seem redundant to talk about faith here, but when we discuss disruptions that deny authorship, we are not talking about faith in Jesus – that is a matter of salvation. Here, we are talking about perspective. I know many Christians, myself included, who have faced a disruption that obscured their view of the providence of God. Disruptions of this type cause us to think that God is unaware or unconcerned with our plight. While we may not walk away from following Christ, it does shift our view of the providence and power of God. The danger with disruptions of this sort is that eventually, they do lead to a disconnection in the relationship. You can walk only so long with a person, not fully trusting them, before you altogether fall out of love with them!

---

[52] John C. Maxwell, *Failing Forward: Turning Mistakes into Stepping-Stones for Success* (Nashville, TN: Thomas Nelson Publishers, 2000), 77.

I will never forget when Karen and I were expecting our fourth child. Our youngest, Jeremiah was 11, but we had three boys and no girl. We prayed and we played (you know I don't see nothin' wrong...), and after about a year, God answered our prayers – Karen was pregnant. I was so excited, I started purchasing baby stuff. I knew it was a girl, because a girl is what I prayed for! Even in preaching, I would make mention of my daughter on the way. Our joy was turned to sorrow, at the end of the first trimester, when we went in for an ultrasound, only to hear that the baby had not survived past the tenth week. It hurt. We grieved. But we did not give up praying! We knew that a healthy pregnancy was no guarantee – Karen was nearly 40 - and we were told that there could be risks. Sometime later, Karen was pregnant again!

You see, God answers prayer. Except this time, it felt like God was an immature prankster. Eight weeks was as long as our joy lasted, and another pregnancy ended in a miscarriage. I will never forget the look in my wife's eyes, as I sat there... scholar...pastor...theologian...with no words to answer, 'Why would God do this to me? TWICE!' She asked me with eyes full of tears, and turned her head away to the hospital wall, as if to say...'It doesn't even matter...I won't ask for a child again!' And she didn't. But thank God that I did. I asked enough for the both of us. Karen got pregnant again! TWICE! And now we have two absolutely gorgeous daughters, Kennedy and Kharis. The point here is that we cannot allow our disruptions to render our faith in the providence of God null and void.

DEFYING THE LEADERSHIP

Once more we hit a disruption that it seems we have already discussed – the divine connection - but this too is something of a different nature. The relationship, that is a matter of salvation. The authorship, that is a matter of trust and perspective. The leadership, this is a matter of submission. These types of disruptions are specifically those that we face after having put our faith in Jesus our savior, but cause us to live a life of rebellion. These disruptions are most often something that has happened *to* us, especially while in service to God. If you have ever been hurt by someone and fought God with all your heart to keep from forgiving them, you are familiar with this disruption. The *good works* that we have been made for, *should* be works that we engage in. Forgiveness is a good work. Humility is a good work. This type of disruption happens often in the church. Perhaps we fail to see the unity in the church that Jesus asked for in John 17, because we fail to walk in obedience in some of the most basic, reconciling, *good works* for which we have been created. Perhaps you are seeing a pattern that most of our disruptions are, in effect 'divine interruptions,' in that they create some type of discontinuity in our work, our walk, or our worship. Disruptions are indeed "one of the most significant challenges to any believer's faith. When pain, grief, persecution, or other forms of suffering strike, we find ourselves caught off guard, confused, and full of questions. Suffering can strain faith to the limits."[53]

A 'DIVINE' INTERRUPTION?

> **Romans 8:37–39 (NASB)**
>
> [37] But in all these things we overwhelmingly conquer through Him who loved us. [38] For I am convinced that neither death, nor life, nor angels, nor principalities, nor things present, nor things to come, nor powers, [39] nor height, nor depth, nor any other created thing, will be able to separate us from the love of God, which is in Christ Jesus our Lord.

*We conquer...nothing can separate...*I can think of several other passages that seem to convey that we should not experience divine interruptions. However, this conclusion would certainly be a misunderstanding of Scripture. What Scripture affirms is that God's love for us is unending and uninterrupted. However, it never promises that our experiences and reflections of that love will never be met with opposition. James Dobson authored an incredible book that is helpful for anyone facing a disruption, entitled *When God Doesn't Make Sense*.[54] In the book, he shares stories, both Biblical and modern, of individuals who experienced trials that seemed to separate them from communion with God. While the separation seems real, he writes to show readers that the love of God has never changed, but warns that "when a person begins to conclude that he or she is disliked or hated by the Almighty, demoralization is not far behind."[55]

---

[53] R. C. Sproul, *Surprised by Suffering: The Role of Pain and Death in the Christian Life* (Lake Mary, FL: Reformation Trust Publishing, 2010), 1.

[54] James Dobson, *When God Doesn't Make Sense* (Wheaton, IL: Tyndale House, 1993).

[55] Dobson, *When God Doesn't Make Sense*, 21.

Further, he assures us that "the Lord can be trusted – even when He can't be tracked."[56] John Piper writes that "the darkest experience for the child of God is when his faith sinks out of his own sight. Not out of God's sight, but his. Yes, it is possible to be so overwhelmed with [disruptions] that you do not know if you are a Christian—and yet still be one."[57] What both of these highly influential spiritual leaders are affirming is the fact we can experience divine interruptions, or disruptions that seem to have an interrupting effect in our divine relationships.

There is, however, another 'divine interruption,' synonymous to this one; same term, different meaning. There is the divine interruption that recognizes the hand of a sovereign, good, loving God in the midst of a disruption. Whereas disruptions can *seem* to contradict the very nature and character of God, we should not conclude that our disruptions are matters beyond the control of God. Piper stated as much when he addressed the COVID-19 pandemic, suggesting that the coronavirus was 'sent by God,' and that "this is not a season for sentimental views of God. It is a bitter season. And God ordained it. God governs it. He will end it. No part of it is outside his sway. Life and death are in his hand."[58]

In the early days of the COVID-19 pandemic, I called the situation a 'divine disruption.' A friend of mine pointed out the connotations that come along with such a term. And, I will be honest... as a preacher, it just sounded so spiritually mature to say! I totally agree with Piper, that no part of this pandemic, (or our personal disruptions) are 'outside his way.' But my friend was right! Many could be turned off to God and to the gospel, for reading that statement as God having desired to see our world suffering as it did. Did I mean that God found pleasure in a virus that was crippling economies, interrupting traditions, and ultimately costing dear lives? By no means! What I was suggesting, Biblically speaking, was that nothing happens outside of the providence of God. Whether it be by desire or allowance, it is still within the power of God.

Three weeks into the COVID-19 Pandemic, pastors had to shift from preaching to live congregations in the church, to preaching to Facebook and

---

[56] Dobson, *When God Doesn't Make Sense*, 21.

[57] John Piper, *When the Darkness Will Not Lift: Doing What We Can While We Wait for God—And Joy* (Wheaton, IL: Crossway Books, 2006), 38.

[58] "Not a season for Sentimental Views of God," in John Piper, *Coronavirus and Christ* (Wheaton, IL: Crossway, 2020), chapter 4, Logos Digital Resource, np.

YouTube audiences. People could not even worship together. *Seriously? The house of God*? How could God possibly allow things to get *this* bad? Many questions began to surface – in homes, in social media, even Bishop T.D. Jakes was called upon to answer questions on mainstream television. The questions that were raised were no different than the questions that we offer up when we are facing disruptions of our own. What is important, in this regard, is that we hold on to several truths: God has all power, God is good, God's creation suffers under the effects of the fall, but God still loves his creation.

GOD HAS ALL POWER

Is God powerful enough to do anything about this? Sometimes the questions that we ask have more to do with his hand (is he able to?) than his mind (does he think he should?) or his heart (does he even want to?). Bottom line, we are wanting to know if our disruption is beyond the control of God. When we speak of God's control, we are ultimately bringing into view God's providence. Jerry Bridges defines God's providence as "His constant care for and His absolute rule over all His creation for His own glory and the good of His people…note the absolute terms: constant care, absolute rule, all creation. Nothing, not even the smallest virus, escapes His care and control."[59] According to R. C. Sproul, it is when we face disruptions that the providence of God becomes one of the most difficult doctrines for Christians to accept.[60]

To say that God has all power is to say that he is fully resourced, and wholly reasonable. How else could he cause all things to work together for good (Romans 8:28)? Psalm 104 is a beautiful psalm that speaks of God's power displayed in both the creation and the care of this world, leading the psalmist to conclude, *'Bless the Lord, O my soul! Praise the Lord!'* We read Biblical narratives, preach sermons, and sing songs that attest to the providence of God. *'He's Able!' 'He can _____ !'* He's bigger than, stronger than, greater than… These are all familiar phrases in our hymns, creeds, poems, and church vernacular. While they may resound through our sanctuaries and church gatherings, the realities of our disruptions bring a deafening blow to these affirmations. If he is bigger, stronger, greater, and able, then how is it, or why is it that we have to endure disruptions? If he

---

[59] Bridges, *Trusting God*, 25.
[60] Sproul, *Surprised by Suffering*, 38.

can, why *won't* he? This is a question that pastors, scholars, and theologians have been trying to satisfactorily answer since the Bible itself was being authored.

What I am calling **DISRUPTIONS** in this book, Bible scholars have rightly labeled suffering and evil. Gerald Bray attempts to address this issue in a clear way, suggesting that

> it is undoubtedly hard to understand how an all-powerful and loving God can permit the continued existence of [disruption] in the world, when presumably he could snuff it out whenever he wanted to, but although this difficulty has haunted Christian theologians from the beginning, it is easier to live with its problems than with those that would be created if his absolute sovereignty were to be denied. A world controlled by God is a world in which he can always act to save us, even if there are forces in it that are prepared to attack and enslave us. If he were not ultimately in control of those forces, we could have no assurance that he is able to help us and could easily find ourselves in the depths of despair.[61]

Jerry Bridges also tries to offer a way forward in considering the providence of God, noting that when we speak of his providence, we encounter a problem, in that

> we either unconsciously or deliberately imply that God intervenes at specific points in our lives but is largely only an interested spectator most of the time. When we think this way, even unconsciously, we reduce God's control over our lives to a stop-and-go, in-and-out proposition. Our unconscious attitude is that the rest of the time we are the "master of our fates" or conversely the victims of unhappy circumstances or uncaring people that cross our paths.[62]

What both of these authors contribute leads us back to chapter one in our discussion of God, and who is in ultimate authority. The conflict then lies in the fact that those who do believe in God, that is – the God of the Bible, believe him to be an all-powerful God who created all that there is,

---

[61] Bray, *God Is Love*, 145.
[62] Bridges, *Trusting God*, 25.

and sustains it by his hands alone (Psalm 104), and realize that we are finite, created beings that can neither rebuke God, nor report him to a higher authority.[63] Those two truths cause our questions to change. It is no longer *'Can't you do anything?'* that we wonder. When our questions begin to sound like those of Job, *'What did I ever do to you?' 'Why are you coming at me like this!?'* (Job 7:20) then we are no longer questioning his hand (power/providence) but we are questioning his heart (love/goodness).[64] But as we will see, God's providence, goodness, and love are unending attributes of God, even in the midst of our disruptions.

GOD IS GOOD

If I had to choose only one of my gadgets, it would be my iPhone 11Pro Max; not because I like talking on the phone... I don't, and I don't care too much for a lot of alerts. I love my phone because it has so many apps in it, that it's like having a digital toolbox and a personal assistant in my pocket. One app that I was once extremely fond of, I have stopped using altogether. One of its features failed me, miserably! Perhaps you've used it. It's the level feature in the compass app. I did away with this app because the level feature actually did not work on its own. I had a major design project that I was working on. I was remodeling a ministry center and had to hang some oversized canvas prints in a particular fashion. The layout was meticulously designed on the computer, so I knew just how much space to put between each poster.

I did not think much of the app asking me to 'calibrate' it before using it to make sure that the posters were level... I just found a flat surface, per the instructions, calibrated it, then used my handy dandy iPhone to hang the posters. Now, you might be thinking, *'If it was an important job, why not use an actual level?'* Fair enough – but I figured it was such an advanced device, that if it said it did something, it should do it. It wasn't until someone walked in the room and criticized how obviously crooked some of the posters were, that the light came on. 'Did you level them as you were hanging them?' they asked. "Of course, I did! This is not my first rodeo!' I so proudly replied. 'What level did you use?!' as they looked at the professional level, lying on the floor. From the top of the scaffolding, I pulled out my shiny new iPhone and waved it. I was stumped at their

---

[63] Bray, *God Is Love*, 144.
[64] Sproul, *Surprised by Suffering*, 38.

question – knowing that I had no witty comeback… 'How do you know THAT is level?!' In order for this app to actually be level, it needed something level to be compared to, and what I used to calibrate it might not have actually been level.

I'm afraid that the same standard seems to apply when we talk about the goodness of God. Now, I know that it is very popular to hear the refrain in our church services, *'God is good!'* with the response, *'All the time!'* and if I said, *'All the time…'*, you might just say, *'God is good!'* But, to what are we comparing HIS goodness? When we say God is good, what do we really mean? Do we mean that God fits within our particular system of beliefs, ideals, prejudices, or moral balances? From a Christian perspective, Bray is absolutely correct, who says that while we can measure our human obedience by our obedience to the commands of God, the same criteria cannot be used for measuring the goodness of God – to whom is God subject? God's goodness "must therefore be something different from what it is in us, even if the way it manifests itself bears some resemblance to what we would recognize as good."[65] Even more, he says

> It is all very well for us to say that God does not kill, commit adultery, steal, or bear false witness against his neighbor, but what do such things mean in his case? Who would God steal from, since everything already belongs to him? What neighbors does he have? How could he commit adultery? If he chooses to kill, that is his right, since whatever he destroys is something he has made (Romans 9:19-23). The simple truth is that the categories by which we measure goodness do not apply to God, either because they are meaningless in his case or because his sovereign power is not subject to any law. For that reason, a checklist of moral precepts, however valid it may be when applied to us, cannot be the standard by which we measure God's goodness.[66]

The fact of the matter is, when we look at goodness we are generally thinking about action. But when we talk about goodness, as it relates to God, this view of goodness would be very limited. God is the plumb line. He is the level by which we make sure our level is straight. His commands are

---

[65] Bray, *God Is Love*, 156.
[66] Bray, *God Is Love*, 157.

birthed from the goodness of his very nature (Psalm 119:68). The goodness of God is not a matter of what he does, rather it is who he is. So, when we say that God is good, we are not talking simply about the activity in which he engages, though they too are good, but we are talking about his existence both in and outside of creation. In fact, in the deepest and truest sense of the word, as we noted in chapter 1, Jesus rightly responded in Mark 10:18, when he said, "Why do you call me good? No one is good except God alone!"

CREATION IS STILL FALLEN

It is rather comical how many times I have complained about something, such as the intensity of labor, or perhaps the hateful attitude that I might display, or just anything that reminds me of the fallen nature of humanity. I do something that you probably do too, if you are a Christian, or have a familiarity with the Genesis account of creation and the fall of humanity. I blame Adam and Eve. I blame them, as if the world would be perfect had they not sinned in the Garden. But can I make such an assumption? Guy Duffield and Nathaniel M. Van Cleave give excellent discussion to this issue, and make a few observations that are quite noteworthy. First, we assume that we *only* sin because of Adam and Eve. We act as if we are victims of what Duffield and Van Cleave call a 'polluted ancestry.'[67] But if polluted ancestry were our excuse for our sin, what ancestry did Adam and Eve have to blame their disobedience on? The reality is that God created humankind to enjoy a fellowship of love, with him and each other (Matthew 22:37-40). Such a fellowship could *only* be made possible if humanity was given free-will.

As exciting as it might have been for us to explore Ephesians 2:10 and realize that we (humankind) were a special part of creation, it is rather sobering to realize that we are the part of his creation that actively destroys all of the rest of his 'good' creation (Genesis 1).[68] Ponder that for a moment. God created nature to evolve in a particular way. It is amazing to watch National Geographic or Animal Planet, and watch how the cycle of life seems to work itself out in a beautiful, natural way. But when humanity begins to interfere with nature, going beyond that of survival to sport and curiosity, we begin to see the cycle lose its balance. The sad reality is that

---

[67] Guy P. Duffield and Nathaniel M. Van Cleave, *Foundations of Pentecostal Theology* (Los Angeles, CA: L.I.F.E. Bible College, 1983), 152.

[68] Bray, *God Is Love*, 72.

sin had (in the Garden) and still has (in the world) distorted man's perspective of life. It has distorted man's view of himself, of God, of humanity, and all the rest of God's creation. Can you even name a place today where the effects of sin are not clearly seen? Even the church is not exempt from its effects. Duffield and Van Cleave wisely note:

> so devastating is the influence of sin upon the human consciousness that now sin is glamorized until it is being recognized in society as the thing to do. A great man once said, "Our greatest defense against sin is to be shocked at it"; and when this attitude ceases, sin has accomplished its direst results.[69]

GOD LOVES HIS CREATION

How great is the Father's love for us! I was reading through the Bible several years back, and decided to take my time. I might read a chapter today, but maybe three verses tomorrow. I wanted to start at the very beginning of the Bible and read it all the way through, taking it all in, deeply. I read through the creation account, and tried my best to imagine each scene. It was in the third chapter when I saw the love of God in a fresh way. Everything he made was good. The only thing he did not think was good was Adam's loneliness. So, Adam gets a custom-made bride. I don't care how great a budget, you cannot make a reality dating show that competes with their love story! At the backdrop of paradise – nothing as beautiful will our eyes ever behold on this side of glory...following the most romantic matchmaking scene *ever*...and as far as spiritual goes – you met with God on the regular, chilling naked in the grass. Adam and Eve had the perfect world! No taxes, no COVID-19, no racial prejudices, no gender confusion. IT. WAS. GOOD. Until they thought good wasn't good enough. They sinned, and the Bible says that their eyes were opened, so they hid when they heard God coming.

Imagine that! This is the first time that God *ever* had to play hide and seek with Adam! Marco...Polo... Granted, God knew exactly where Adam was. Reminds me of my three-year-old daughter, Kennedy, who would sometimes 'hide' in her pop-up tent when it was time for bed. Every time I yelled 'Where's Kennedy?!' I'd hear the cutest little snicker, but I

---

[69] Duffield and Van Cleave, *Pentecostal Theology*, 167.

couldn't dare reveal that I knew where she was. In the same way, God entertained the naivete of Adam, and asked, 'Where are you?' While this might not seem like an inquisition of love to some, I would argue that it is indeed a love language of sorts. It was perhaps exactly what Adam wanted to hear in that moment. Those three questions in Genesis 3:9-11, *where, who,* and *what*, indicate the types of questions that bring us the most comfort in our disruptions. *Where are you?* helps me feel that my presence is missed. *Who told you…?* suggests that my assessment of my condition might not be accurate. *Have you…?* indicates that you are concerned with the actions that I have taken. God interrupts Adam's shame and embarrassment with what I would call *corrective love inquisition*. He asks questions that validate the communion that they had, and that which (through Christ) they may once again enjoy.

The questions could have been altogether different! God could have avoided questions all around, and simply expelled them from the Garden. Better yet, he put Adam to sleep once… God could have doubled down on the whole nap time gig, and reset humanity with Arthur and Evelyn. But that is not the history of redemption; what was said was said. But his love extended beyond words. Love transitioned from dialogue to demonstration. Genesis 3:8 records that Adam and Even hid themselves from the presence of the Lord. Although we read about thirteen verses of dialogue between God and his fallen children, we never receive the report that they 'unhid' themselves. What shame and sorrow must they have felt as they spoke with their father, pastor, mentor, matchmaker, interior and exterior designer…and now, their personal haberdasher? Genesis 3:21 says that God looked at their efforts to cover up their shame (their nakedness), and saw that it was inadequate. So, while they were in the thick of their sin and shame, he still loved them enough to provide for them a more excellent covering. He upgraded their fig leaf garments for them.

I love the picture that I had in mind when I read this verse. It says that God made garments, *and clothed them*. Now having read this verse many times before, I read the second part of the sentence as an explanation of the first. But literally, it says that God made clothes for them, and put them on Adam and Eve. That is love in the most beautiful sense; that God not only provided what was necessary to cover their shame, but he put it where it needed to go. This is most beautifully and fully seen in the life *and* the death of Jesus. God's love is seen in Genesis just as vividly as it is seen in the gospels. God provided what was needed to cover our sin and our shame when the virgin Mary became pregnant with child. Jesus the Messiah, who lived a sinless life – that was what we needed. But even that Jesus, at the lowest point of his humanity, said to the Father, 'I know I am what they need... but *please,* don't put me where they need me... *nevertheless...*' (Matthew 26:36-42). Jesus knew that *he* was a more excellent covering for our sins than bulls and goats (the sacrificial animals used in the Old Testament). But he also knew where he would need to be placed – not on our shoulders like garments, but on the cross, like the two thieves between whom he was hanged.

Perhaps we do not find difficulty in holding to an acceptance of God's love. Those of us who have surrendered our lives to the Lordship of Jesus confess as much in our affirmation that he gave his life freely for the remission of our sins. But in reality, disruptions have an uncanny way of eclipsing the work of Jesus on the cross: the untimely death of a loved one; the sudden loss of a job; the collapse of an economy that leaves a benevolent Christ-follower to have to consider welfare, bankruptcy, or suffer homelessness; the family that is adversely impacted by the effects of a violent crime. All of these and more can lead one to ask, 'How would a loving God allow this to happen?' I have personally found two thoughts about the love of God to be helpful in the midst of disruptions.

> God's love is sovereign; that His powerful arm is also His arm of tender care. But it seems so often we do not *see* or *sense* God's sovereign love exercised on our behalf. Instead, we see ourselves beset with all kinds of calamities that come rolling in upon us. We see ourselves as the victims of "nature's cruel fate", of the injustices of other people, and of adversities that occur with no rational cause. It is at times like this that we must take our stand by faith on the assurances of God's love given to us in the Scriptures.[70]

> God's willingness to preserve the fallen spiritual creatures in spite of their rebellion is matched by his desire to keep the human race in being. This is a mystery that can be explained only by his deep love for his creatures. Looked at in a purely rational light, it would not have been

---

[70] Bridges, *Trusting God*, 147.

surprising if God had decided to wipe us out and start again. A master potter does not tolerate a flawed vase and will either smash it or rework it. The Bible reminds us that we are pottery in God's hands and that he has made us without consulting us first.[71]

As difficult as it may be for us to reconcile the relationships between God's sovereignty, his love, and our disruptions, the truth of the matter is we are his, all that exists is his, and he knows what he's doing with what is his. Sometimes, things look bad. Who am I kidding? Sometimes things absolutely *are* bad! But even *bad* things are never out of his control!

DISRUPTIONS ARE 'THINGS'

> **Romans 8:26–28 (NASB)**
>
> [26] In the same way the Spirit also helps our weakness; for we do not know how to pray as we should, but the Spirit Himself intercedes for us with groanings too deep for words; [27] and He who searches the hearts knows what the mind of the Spirit is, because He intercedes for the saints according to the will of God. [28] And we know that God causes all things to work together for good to those who love God, to those who are called according to His purpose.

Here is the proof. It is not our intellect, our resources, our experiences, nor our social capital that cause things to work together for good; it is the one who *is* eternally, unshakably good – God! Because it is *God* who is causing it all to work together, we can be confident that

> we never face any assault of flesh, devil, circumstance or personal weakness without God's hand present, mighty and available to work through it all—and beyond it all. This doesn't mean God has planned every bad thing that happens to people. Evil things that are initiated by hell's hatefulness or by human sin, failure and rebellion create

---

[71] Bray, *God Is Love*, 473.

their own problems. But beyond them all, God's ultimate deliverance is our promised inheritance.[72]

Jerry Bridges says that the 'things' that this verse speaks of are like the ingredients of biscuit dough; alone they are undesirable, and neither do we care for the heat which comes from the oven, but when it all comes together, the end result is something that we appreciate.[73] Isn't it interesting that God orchestrates events in the same fashion in which he has created us? We were created to do good works (Ephesians 2:10) and in the course of these good works, this passage makes it evident that we are going to encounter disruptions that we don't have the natural strength to make it through. That *the Spirit helps in our weakness* suggests that there are things that God's special creation who are created for good works will sometimes encounter, and not have the mental, physical, emotional, spiritual, or other capacity to overcome. In these situations, because he is powerful, good, and loving, he has made ready an advocate – *The Spirit*, who intercedes, or prays specifically and intelligently for us. Look how informed the prayer is... *according to the will of God*!

Have you ever just found yourself trying to pray, and felt like you were just rambling? You were praying, wondering, 'Is this the right thing to be asking for?' or wondering, 'Is this the right time to be asking for this?' We especially want to be mature in our disruptions, praying just as Jesus did in the garden of Gethsemane, *"Lord, I'm good if you'd get me out of this...like now!'* but, we often leave out the '*...but, nevertheless, not my will, but yours.'* None of that exists in this prayer which is prayed by the Spirit of God! Paul says that the Spirit prays *according to the will of God*! That means all the right words, for all the right reasons, at all the right times!

It is for *this* reason that we have hope in our disruptions. Do you see, now, why the God that we place our hope in is significant, as we discussed in the first chapter? God the Father, sent God the Son, who would then send God the Spirit, after his resurrection, which gives us an all-around solution to facing disruptions. What an amazing hope that we have, even when we cannot understand why we are going through the things that we face (be it a global pandemic, or a personal crisis), that no one shares in but us.

---

[72] Jack W. Hayford, *Hope for a Hopeless Day: Encouragement and Inspiration When You Need It Most* (Ventura, CA: Regal; Gospel Light, 2007), 82–83.
[73] Bridges, *Trusting God*, 152.

A.W. Tozer offers a great illustration to fully appreciate how God works, even in our disruptions, no matter how painful, how complicated, and even how unfair. He tells the story of the hammer and the nail:

> The hammer is a useful tool, but the nail, if it had feeling and intelligence, could present another side of the story. For the nail knows the hammer only as an opponent, a brutal, merciless enemy who lives to pound it into submission, to beat it down out of sight and clinch it into place. That is the nail's view of the hammer, and it is accurate except for one thing: The nail forgets that both it and the hammer are servants of the same workman. Let the nail but remember that the hammer is held by the workman and all resentment toward it will disappear. The carpenter decides whose head shall be beaten next and what hammer shall be used in the beating. That is his sovereign right. When the nail has surrendered to the will of the workman and has gotten a little glimpse of his benign plans for its future, it will yield to the hammer without complaint.[74]

If you and I really surrendered to the reality that the same 'carpenter' who created us is the very one who is actively present in all the events that take place in our lives, we might see our disruptions in a brand-new light. We must remember, he engages even that which he did not engineer; as Joseph said to his brothers, who had devised a horrible scheme against him, that set in motion a chain of personal disruptions for their young brother, what had been meant for evil, *'God meant (or made it work) for good.'* Pastor John Gunn is a dear friend and mentor. In his five decades of ministry and pastoring, including founding The Power Company Kids Club, where I now pastor, he has experienced disruptions, both personal and in the ministry. I will never forget his words of wisdom to me, when asked how he maintains hope and focus when he as gone through disruptions. "I live my life by two pillar convictions…" he said to me. "The first is a conviction that I am being obedient to the calling (assigned work) of God, and the second is that all that I have (possessions, people, and position), I don't own – it belongs to God; I am a steward." What anchoring conviction to carry you through disruptions!

---

[74] A.W. Tozer, *The Root of the Righteous* (Camp Hill, Pennsylvania: Christian Publications, 1955), 134-35.

WHAT ARE YOU DOING?

> A disruption is any hardship (event, action, word, or thought) which has the effect of temporarily or permanently distorting the workmanship (person), disconnecting the relationship (created in Christ), dismantling the craftsmanship (to do *good* works), denying the authorship (*God* prepared beforehand), and defying leadership (that we *should* walk in them) that our life ought to reflect.

Let us consider this definition once more. I close this chapter with what I argue is the over-arching question that we need to ask ourselves whenever we are facing a disruption of *any* type. Whether it be a global pandemic that has led to months of social distancing, closure of certain recreational spaces, and distance learning, or a personal health, financial, marital, or moral crisis; the most forward-moving question we can ask ourselves is, *'What am I doing!?'* I don't argue that this is the *only* question, nor the only *important* question; quite the contrary! There are several critical questions that are to be asked and answered when we are facing disruptions, but *this* question is the *gateway* question; it is the conductor of the interrogative symphony which will come. Nevertheless, it is *what we do* in the midst of a disruption that will most certainly inform what is the outcome of the disruption; therefore, we must make this question our 'ground zero.'

Are you waiting? Are you rehearsing the events that got you where you are? Are you retreating to a place of isolation and seclusion? What are you doing? It is our answer(s) to this question that informs the next leg of our journey when the disruption passes... and it will pass! Ecclesiastes 3 tells us that there is a time and season for *everything* under the sun - that includes our disruptions. What will be your assessment of the disruption season, after it passes? Will you look back on that time with disdain and regret? Will it seem as though you were robbed of precious time? Or will it be a time that you reflect with amazement as you ponder the growth, maturity, and purpose that came out of that time? Over the next four chapters, we explore some common 'doings' and their subsequent outcomes, and learn from Scripture how we can be active participants in God's causing our disruption(s) to work together for good!

QUESTIONS FOR REFLECTION

1. Which of the four hardships listed in our definition (event, action, word, thought) is most familiar to you?

2. Early in the chapter, I note that hardships can lead to identity crises. What are some of the disorienting effects that hardships have had on your sense of identity and self worth?

3. How can a distorted view of self impact any relationship we might seek to have with Christ?

4. What are some ways that good works (acts/actions with social benefit) are impacted by disruptions, in your experience?

5. Concerning authorship (God is in control of 'this') and leadership (God is in control of 'me'), which of the two do you find most interrupted when facing a disruption?

6. God's power, goodness, and love are generally called into question when we face disruptions. Which do you question less when facing disruptions? What helps you to find confidence in this attribute of God?

3 DELAY: WHAT ARE YOU WAITING FOR?

Me and all my friends, we're all misunderstood.
They say we stand for nothing,
and there's no way we ever could.
Now we see everything that's going wrong
with the world and those who lead it.
We just feel like we don't have the means
to rise above and beat it.
So, we keep waiting (waiting)...
Waiting on the world to change!
(John Mayer, 'Waiting on the World to Change,' 2006)

WAITING ON THE WORLD TO CHANGE

I have heard that song time and time again, but never took careful thought of the words. The very reason that John and his friends are waiting is that they feel powerless. Those who are familiar with this song know that it speaks of political issues and war, but the lyrics are the same for us in our disruptions. In this song, the singer acknowledges an authority, or authorities, greater than himself; the world, and those who lead it. Careful attention unveils a key worldview (as we discussed earlier) of the writer. The singer is waiting for *the world* to change. As we listen to the song in its entirety, we get a fuller understanding of what he is talking about. He is waiting for soldiers to return from war, which ultimately means waiting for peace. He is waiting for more integrity in (*social*) media; for honest and open reports about what is taking place in the world.

Ultimately, waiting for an opportunity for him and '(*his*) *generation*' to one day have seats of authority in this world gone wrong. In other words, waiting for them to one day be named among '*those who lead*' the world. It assumes that the rest of the world would then share in his political, social, religious, and economic views. What he is essentially awaiting is not for the world to *change*, but for the world to *conform* to his view of right and wrong. While these words are not expressed by the author himself, they can certainly be understood from the words he writes.

What this song helps to illustrate is the fact that waiting is our way of delegating authority in a matter. When we find ourselves waiting, whomever (or whatever) it is that we are waiting on has the ultimate authority. Let's enter the laboratory of life for a moment, and see if this hypothesis rings true. First, we must agree to terms here; by 'waiting' I am using this term in the most direct manner, based on *Webster's Dictionary,* which suggests that the word means to "stay where one is or delay action until a particular time or until something else happens."[75] Consider some of the most common waiting scenarios, and note the authority figures:

SCENARIO	AUTHORITY FIGURE(S)	BASIS OF AUTHORITY
Waiting at a red light	Transit authority, law enforcement, traffic light timer	You cannot *legally* continue without a green light.
Waiting for medical results	The doctor, the lab tech, the lab equipment	You cannot circumvent their procedure to satisfy your need to know.
Waiting for someone to apologize	The offender	As long as you are *waiting* for an apology, the issue is unresolved; the offender decides if and when resolution happens.
Waiting for the weekend!	God, the clock, employer, the parent(s) of your child(ren)/grandchildren, and the list goes on!!!	Regardless of what is meant by 'the weekend,' you have no control over time – you can only manage what time you are given.
Waiting for the mail.	Mail carrier, package sender	You have no power over the arrival of this package, only tracking and waiting.

Traffic lights, television commercials, customer service; these are trivial examples to paint a much bigger picture. Think of disruptions that

---

[75] 'Wait,' *Webster's Dictionary.*

take place in our lives. Disruptions in the marriage. Disruptions on the job. Physical disruptions. Emotional disruptions. Who is in control? What is in control? The people or things that we wait for are the people and things to which we are relinquishing control. It is clear then that we cannot simply sit by *waiting for the world to change*. In fact, it is specifically *because* the world is ever-changing that we cannot wait for the world.

We cannot wait for people, because we ourselves understand that people can be driven by their own emotions, opinions, ideals, and even prejudices. Waiting for people certainly cannot be a viable option. If "our interpretations of life are influenced by our past experiences, our present frame of mind, and our vision of the future,"[76] how unstable and unpredictable an option must it be to wait on people when we are facing disruptions? How distorted would one's actions or instructions be toward us in the midst of a disruption if their interpretation was based solely on their past experiences? What about basing them on their (limited) witness of *our* past experiences? Even in professional services, such as the medical or legal fields, while experience does inform their actions, there is always the fine print that says they can make no particular guarantees, based on these things. Our present state of mind today may be much different than it was yesterday; it is certainly much different than it was three years ago! My vision for the future, while somewhat fixed (or so it seems), still has the potential to change at the micro level. Simply put, people change, so there is no sense in *waiting* for people to change!

Things change; therefore, waiting for things to change is equally problematic, both physically and figuratively. The old adage, *time heals all wounds* is far from true. If anything, time *reveals* all wounds! Most often, the 'things' that we are waiting for to change are intangible things; they are situational things. We are waiting for our work environment to change. We wait for our finances to be in order. We wait for certain laws to pass. As I write this chapter, millions of American citizens are waiting for their COVID-19 stimulus check to arrive, and countless others are waiting for their approved unemployment compensation. Families are waiting at home for the news that their loved ones, lying alone in the hospital at the mercy of the Coronavirus, are turning the corner for the better. Others have given up hope and are awaiting the call that things took a turn for the worse. While

---

[76] Gary Chapman, *Covenant Marriage: Building Communication & Intimacy* (Nashville, TN: Broadman & Holman Publishers, 2003), 65.

the world navigates a global crisis, students are waiting for things to get back to normal so that they can finally have classes in person. Some are waiting to escape crises they were navigating before the world stood still. While all of these waiting scenarios are completely logical and understandable, the fact still remains – we have relinquished control.

I remember pulling into the driveway and sitting in my truck. I probably sat for twenty minutes. I was waiting. I was waiting for the right words to say to my bride of just over two years. I was trying to figure out how I would communicate the news. Not only were we newlyweds but we were also new parents. Our eldest son, Aaron, was just over a year old, and Karen was pregnant with our second son, Isaiah. After waiting for so long, the words really never came to me. So instead of waiting for words to say, I was waiting to wake up. Maybe this was all a dream. Maybe I was having a random nightmare, and I just needed the alarm to go off. So, I waited. I waited for words. I waited to wake up. *I was just waiting… waiting… waiting for my world to change.*

That morning started out differently. Generally, I would have to be at work by 7:45, but that day, I was told to come to our home office before reporting to the worksite. I worked as a contractor in one of the 'Big Three' automotive groups in the Metro Detroit area. As a hardware engineer, it was my job to install, service, and upgrade computers and workstations for engineers in the building. I did my job considerably well. I enjoyed many times of laughter and great conversations with my team. I was the newest on the team and was paid the least, so you can imagine that I worked as if I had something to prove. In fact, my supervisor (who was also a contractor but from another firm), had recently spoken with me about switching to their agency in order to earn better pay. These are, in part, reasons why this morning was exceptionally bizarre for me.

The day previous, I received a call from my contracting headquarters. My contract manager wanted me to come by the main office before I reported to work. I remember coming home, excited to tell Karen that they wanted to meet with me in the morning. I had been working for them for almost a year. It was my second assignment through the agency, and I was specifically requested to be assigned to that second job, because the supervisor on site saw my work ethic when I was just delivering computers to them. Surely this meeting was supposed to be the next level meeting; I was confident that they were going to talk about a pay raise, or even a promotion. The meeting was the exact opposite.

I was told of a number of allegations in regard to my work performance, and even accused of insubordination. I was instructed that I would no longer be able to step foot on the premises, and that all of my belongings would be mailed to me. I would not even be escorted by a guard to clean out my own personal articles from my cubicle. Simply put, I was terminated from that contract, and after tearfully and humbly defending every accusation, was assured that they would find me another contract. Although the accusations did not add up to my contract manager (they were far from descriptive of the Aaron Robinson this company had come to know – even in such a short time), I handed her my badge, and took the long way home. So, there I was in my driveway… waiting… wondering… worrying… maybe even wishing (in the most negative way imaginable)! Finally, I had to go into the house and give Karen the news.

I'll never forget. She was still in bed asleep. It was early, and she had not expected me to return so soon. I sat silently on the edge of the bed breathing heavily, waiting. Waiting for her to ask what's wrong. Waiting for a call from my contract manager to interrupt this moment with news that my former supervisor repented of the allegations. I waited. Karen must have been waiting also, because she never sat up and asked a question. I would have to open my mouth with courage and simply tell my wife what was going on. I told her the long version of the meeting, every grueling detail, bawling my eyes out the entire time. As she sat, silently, it made me cry more! I could only imagine what she was thinking.

Karen responded, with faith-filled optimism, that perhaps God had a plan for all of this. She even brought up the idea of working for myself. Although I was generally the one in the marriage who saw God at work, this was not one of those times. Her encouraging response may have softened the blow of the job loss, but I was not quite ready to 'rise and shine and give God the glory!' I hadn't even been married for three years yet! I had one son, and another on the way. I just purchased a big, eight passenger, gas guzzling sport utility vehicle with the biggest engine available, and gas was almost $3 a gallon. I could not see the light at the end of this tunnel! How were we going to get through this? We had no big savings; no nest egg. If there is one word that sums up my reaction to this disruption, it is *waiting*.

First, I waited for the situation to change. As I said, I was waiting for repentance and an apology to come from my former supervisor. I knew that the accusations were unwarranted. I could not understand how a faithful, joyful, committed employee could be so maliciously attacked. I knew…I just knew somehow that this was all going to pan out to be a big misunderstanding or something. I waited for an opportunity to tell my story. I waited for someone to ask me what happened with that job. Every time the opportunity came to share my story, still nothing changed. I waited for some of my former coworkers to call me and tell me how they found out what happened, and how unfair it was. Those calls did indeed come, but after hours of talking with other guys from the team who voiced their concerns and their outrage, nothing changed. I waited for unemployment to kick in. The little money that I made through unemployment barely helped ends meet. I waited on another call for another assignment. No call ever came.

Have you ever had a disruption where all you could do was wait? Have you ever had something take place in your life and the only question that ran through your mind was *'When*?' That is exactly where I was. Eventually I realized one of the greatest lessons that I could learn when dealing with disruptions. In all of my waiting, nothing was changing. In fact, the more that I waited like this, the more that my family would be in want. As long as I waited to tell my story, or the longer that I waited for vengeance of any sort…as long as I simply waited for the next job assignment, I would not progress, not in my family, not in my purpose, not in my career. The only thing that waiting of this type accomplished was delaying the purpose that God had for my life.

Something had to change! The problem was, I had no idea what to change. All of the emotions were still there! I was still hurt, confused, angry, and honestly a little scared. I hope to make the lesson that I ultimately learned evidently clear in this chapter. Waiting is not a problem. Waiting is not a sin. Waiting is not an indicator that you don't have faith, or trust God. The problem is not *that* we wait, it is *how* we wait, and the *object* for which we are waiting.

The Bible speaks very clearly on the issue of waiting. One of the saddest, and yet most triumphant stories in the Bible is the story of Job. It is a long book of what most would call undeserved suffering; yet what's saddest about the book is the waiting. One third of the way through the book, the man has waited just about as much as he could stand, and he's finally just waiting to die. At least if he dies, he won't have to go through all this again; so, he waits while he continues to suffer every day (Job 14:14). For forty-one chapters, we get front row seats to waiting gone wrong! It is not until the final chapter that Job reorients his waiting. It is amazing to see how swift the change of his disruption's outcome when he learned to truly wait on God.

WAITING ON GOD: THE EXAMPLES

> **Job 42:1–6 (NASB)**
>
> 1 Then Job answered the Lord and said, [2] "I know that You can do all things, And that no purpose of Yours can be thwarted. [3] 'Who is this that hides counsel without knowledge?' "Therefore I have declared that which I did not understand, Things too wonderful for me, which I did not know." [4] 'Hear, now, and I will speak; I will ask You, and You instruct me.' [5] "I have heard of You by the hearing of the ear; But now my eye sees You; [6] Therefore I retract, And I repent in dust and ashes."

If you read the Bible from cover to cover, you will repeatedly find the command (specifically from God) to wait. It might be of no surprise to you what he commands people to wait for; he says to wait for him! Numerous times, it is affirmed through the psalmists, prophets, kings, and other followers of God, that there are benefits to waiting on him. The prophet Jeremiah, who endured considerable amounts of disruptions in his life exclaimed, "The LORD is good to those who wait for Him, To the person who seeks Him!" (Lamentations 3:25). David, the great shepherd and king of the Old Testament probably has the most to say about waiting on God.

The Old Testament shares story after story of David's disruptions: overlooked by his father; an annoyance to his brothers; underestimated by the king; taunted by a giant; anointed and not yet appointed; hated by a king; hunted by a king; lusted after a married woman; killed a man; lost a child; almost lost the Ark of the Covenant of God; could not keep his family together. The list goes on! David's life would rival the best of our 21st century late night steamy cable television shows! Some of his disruptions were of his own doing, and some were simply the effects of the Fall. Yet David's life is a great example of waiting! The Psalms record some his most intimate waiting moments.

David delighted in waiting on God, and sang "You are the God of my salvation; For You I wait all the day." (Psalm 25:5). Just before these words, he insisted that waiting on God is nothing to be ashamed of – he boasts in it (Psalm 25:3). Later, he suggests that this waiting has provided somewhat of a moral compass for him (Psalm 25:21). He knew that the reward for waiting on God would be much more satisfying than his temporary pleasure. I had a friend who was seeking to lose a certain amount of weight. He never got on the scale; instead, he went to a local menswear store and purchased a suit that was tailored to the size he ultimately wanted to be. That suit hung in his bedroom for months, motivating him to eat healthy and maintain his workout regimen. Each time he wanted to skip leg day, or go for an extra slice of pizza, he remembered his suit. So was the case for David. The promises and the character of God hung as a reminder of what was in store, should he wait.

In Psalm 27:14, David commands that we ought to wait for the Lord. He acknowledges that waiting for God is not always easy, encouraging the listener to "Be strong and let your heart take courage." He pens these words amidst a host of other emotions and experiences. He's writing from a place of fear, depression, abandonment, and loneliness. He's even writing from a place of obedience! He's waiting on God, and argues before the Lord, *"when You said, "Seek My face," my heart said to You, "Your face, O LORD, I shall seek""* (Psalm 27:8). Andrew Murray is absolutely right when he says that "one of the chief needs in our waiting upon God, one of the deepest secrets of its blessedness and blessing, is a quiet, confident persuasion that it is not in vain; courage to believe that God will hear and help; we are waiting on a God who never could disappoint His people."[77]

Because David knew that comparison and anxiety are foes of waiting, David instructs his listeners to "rest in the LORD and wait patiently for Him; Do not fret because of him who prospers in his way." (Psalm 37:7). How many times have you been in a disruption and watched as others seemed to be doing well in those same areas? When I ran my media company, I would be hired to do weddings, and Karen would come along and help me with the photography. I remember one of the weddings we were shooting just made us miserable. It was hard to watch this young couple celebrate this romantic day, knowing that we were waiting for God to intervene in our own marriage in various ways. Truthfully, we were not waiting on each other. We were just waiting… (waiting)… waiting on each other to change.

---

[77] Andrew Murray, *Waiting on God! Daily Messages for a Month* (New York; Chicago; Toronto: Fleming H. Revell, 1896), 45–46.

In Psalm 37:34, David says that we are to "wait for the LORD and keep His way," which means that waiting on the Lord must be intimately connected to the Word of God. In 62:5, he commands his *soul* to wait on God *in silence*, which means that waiting is not just a mental thing, and not always a vocal thing. Sometimes, we just need to be quiet and meditate. Dick Eastman calls such waiting "wordless worship" or "silent surrender", and describes it as "a spiritual love affair with intimate supernatural union."[78] How often do we make waiting on God just a matter of thinking and not something that every part of us, *our very soul* must participate in? Have you ever had a disruption that robbed you of your sleep? Psalm 119:147 says that even if we are tired and emotional, we can still wait on the Lord. Over and over again in Scripture we see the command to wait! Perhaps the most often quoted passage on waiting is found in the book of Isaiah:

> **Isaiah 40:31 (NASB)**
> Yet those who wait for the LORD will gain new strength; they will mount up *with* wings like eagles, they will run and not get tired, they will walk and not become weary. Those who hopefully wait for Me will not be put to shame.

One action: wait on God. One promise: gain new strength. Three evidenced results of this renewed strength: mounting up with wings like eagles, running without getting tired, and walking without becoming weary. I must be honest, familiarity with Bible passages has caused me to read this verse too fast, and not find refuge in the richness of what it is saying. Does this passage speak of simply sitting silently in prayer? Does it mean to cease and desist from all activities until we have heard an audible voice from heaven? Does it mean waiting until a preacher or some spiritual person gives us a prophetic 'word from God' on a matter? I don't offer these suggestions to make light of any of these scenarios, all of which have merit. But how should we interpret the command to wait, and what ought we expect to be the visible results of a renewed strength?

Let us take another deep dive into Scripture, in order that we might appreciate more fully the benefit of waiting on God. First, we should notice

---

[78] Dick Eastman, *The Hour That Changes the World: A Practical Plan for Personal Prayer* (Grand Rapids, MI: Chosen, 2002), 38.

the context right before this rich Scripture. The Lord recognizes disruptions, but reminds Israel that even in the midst of a disruption, he is still the all-powerful God who is not a victim of their disruption; it does not weary him, nor does it confuse his wisdom for the matter. On the contrary, he extends his inability to tire in the midst of a disruption to his creation, which he so dearly loves. For humanity does indeed grow weary. It is not simply a matter of aging; God is very clear here – young, vigorous men grow weary, to the point of stumbling. The language here is so descriptive. They don't just stumble, they stumble *badly*. Before any promise of a renewed strength, a deep comparison is made here, lest the creation (humanity) mistakenly think that they can navigate turbulent times without the creator (God).

> **Isaiah 40:27–30 (NASB)**
>
> [27] Why do you say, O Jacob, and assert, O Israel, "My way is hidden from the LORD, And the justice due me escapes the notice of my God"? [28] Do you not know? Have you not heard? The Everlasting God, the LORD, the Creator of the ends of the earth does not become weary or tired. His understanding is inscrutable. [29] He gives strength to the weary, and to *him who* lacks might He increases power. [30] Though youths grow weary and tired, and vigorous young men stumble badly…

Conjunctions are sometimes the most powerful words in Scripture. I can remember taking Biblical language courses in seminary, and we weren't even allowed to call them conjunctions. *If, and, but, or, yet…* they were more than mere *conjunctions*, we had to call them *discourse markers*. They were the magic that made the passage come alive. Remember the old *Schoolhouse Rock* song, 'Conjunction junction, what's your function?' There was a line that said, in response to this question, 'hooking up two boxcars and making 'em run right.' In verse 31 of this chapter, we have a word that makes the whole thing 'run right'… the word 'yet.' This would suggest that the previous verses are absolutely true, but what will be said next has the power of negation – it can override that truth. By dividing this passage up into three sections, I want to offer practical Biblical insight on three things in particular: (1) *Exercise:* How we wait on God; (2) *Effect:* What waiting on God produces; (3) *Evidence:* How do we know that it is working. Let us begin with the exercise.

THEY THAT WAIT: THE EXERCISE OF WAITING

THOSE WHO WAIT ON THE LORD

Why is it that we find it so difficult to wait on God? Could it be that we really do not understand what it is that we are waiting *for*? Perhaps we have no idea what to do, in the most practical sense of the word. We resemble Ricky Bobby, in the movie Talladega Nights, who appeared startled whenever on camera for an interview, admitting, 'I don't know what to do with my hands!?' We've surveyed a number of passages that encourage us to wait, and will encounter many more if we peruse the Scriptures further. The question remains, *'What does waiting actually look like in practice?'* Such is especially the question when we are in the midst of a disruption! When the world around us is dark and hope seems lost, how do I wait on God?

Consider the goalie and the gardener; two individuals whose very vocation is the task of waiting. Oftentimes, our waiting on God is like the waiting of the goalie. Ever just watch a hockey game or a soccer match? The goalie has a pretty important job. The game rises and falls on his or her ability to defend the goal. The job of a goalie is predominantly waiting. I couldn't do it. I would get too distracted or too comfortable in a resting position while all of the activity is at the other end of the field or rink. Whether the goalie is good or terrible at their job, the fact remains: most of their job is waiting for the action to come to them. Until the game moves toward their goal, they are mere spectators. Cheering spectators, calculating spectators, perhaps even active spectators as they watch the action move back and forth. But they are spectators nonetheless. This is not to minimize their role by any means! The spectator will become the defender, but not until the ball or the puck comes near. Until then, their waiting offers no advancement to the game.

The waiting of the gardener is different. The gardener cannot afford to wait for the action to come, because they know that the action of greatest consequence is unseen. The most vital action is taking place in the darkest place – below the surface. The gardener trusts that the soil, the seed, the moisture, and the sun are working together. But for the seed to return a crop, he or she must work diligently, intentionally, without neglect. Water must be provided. Weeds must be eradicated, boundaries must be set, lest the budding seed become prey to pests of many sorts. For the gardener, waiting is indeed an active task. The gardener's waiting offers the possibility of life to the seed.

Our waiting is perhaps driven and informed by Psalm 46:10, which is commonly translated to '*be still* and know that I am God.' The *New American Standard* renders a more favorable reading... '*cease striving*, and know that I am God.' The passage is speaking of God's people fighting battles that God can fight, simply by speaking a word with his powerful voice (see verse 6). Waiting and being still are not always synonymous. Granted, there are times in our waiting when we must be still. However, being still should be the exception and not the rule. The passage here does not speak to inactivity, but faith and expectation. Waiting on God is first and foremost placing active trust in the person and the presence of God.

By 'active trust,' I mean that we are readying ourselves to receive that which we expect. Waiting on God, in its purest sense, is a matter of stewardship. Think of some of the most blessed moments of waiting in your life. I remember waiting for our wedding date to arrive, after proposing to Karen. In no way was that waiting inactive. We shopped, we planned, we looked at homes, we picked out dishware. Preparations were being made based on our expectancy. When we found out that Karen was pregnant with our first child, we waited to know the gender; but that waiting was an active waiting. What would we name it, if it is a girl? What if it is a boy? Which room in the house would we turn into a nursery? Our waiting demanded an active response – this is stewardship. Waiting on God demands the same, even more from us.

There is a grand difference in active hope, and active trust; the one anticipates, and the other rests. Although the two can, and most often do coexist, we would do well to take notice of the difference. To hope in the Lord is to anticipate the fulfillment of his promises and the display of his power. When we hope in the Lord, we are ultimately expecting something. Thus Hebrews 11:1 explains that 'faith is the assurance of things hoped for, the conviction of things not seen.' Trust, however, is different – when we trust in God, we do not anticipate what *will be*, we rest in what is. We find evidence of this in Proverbs 3:5–6, where we are instructed to 'Trust in the LORD with all your heart and do not lean on your own understanding. In all your ways acknowledge Him, And He will make your paths straight.' The leaning and acknowledging that this passage speaks of is a perfect example of active trust. To lean is to rest, but that resting is not inactive, for the very next verse makes that clear – *in all your ways*, in other words, in all that you are *doing*. To acknowledge him means to pay close attention, study, recognize him. We may hope in the promise that *'he will... '* but we must first trust.

Hope puts in view the ability of God, and trust is more concerned with the attributes of God. It is only by first placing an active trust in who God says he is, and the truth that he delights in his creation, that we can place any real assurance in anything that he can and or will do on our behalf. Too often, we hope without trusting. Hope of this sort leaves us disappointed because our expectations are not founded on anything concrete. We hope that God will heal, without fully trusting that he is a healer. We expect him to deliver, placing no trust in the fact that he can. How then, in the most practical sense, are we to wait on God? The answer can be sung to the tune of the old 1887 hymn, written by John H. Sammis, which commands to 'Trust and Obey'.

> *When we walk with the Lord in the light of his Word,*
> *What a glory he sheds on our way.*
> *While we do his good will, he abides with us still,*
> *and with all who will trust and obey*

Waiting on the Lord is a combination of walking, working, trusting, and obeying. We walk with the Lord in our daily communion with him. For many of us, the problem is that we battle a 'hurry sickness,' in which "we are haunted by the fear that there are just not enough hours in the day to do what needs to be done. We will read faster, talk faster, and when listening, nod faster to encourage the talker to accelerate. We will find ourselves chafing whenever we have to wait."[79] Waiting is not a hurried action; it is a pace. Waiting is a daily practice of communion with God. This practice should be done in an intentional and deliberate way. Perhaps it is taking a year and reading through a daily devotional Bible, or taking advantage of the many 14-day or 30-day Bible reading plans that are available in most Bible reading apps today. But we must start with pacing ourselves in our walk with God.

Second, we must work. Remember that we were created for good works, which means that even while we wait, we wait on purpose – with purpose. How do we know what good work to do? We are given clear

---

[79] John Ortberg, *The Life You've Always Wanted: Spiritual Disciplines for Ordinary People* (Grand Rapids, MI: Zondervan, 1997), Kindle location, 1139.

instructions in Micah 6:8; that '[God] has told you, O man, what is good; and what does the LORD require of you but to do justice, to love kindness, and to walk humbly with your God?' As we daily draw near to God in devotional communion, we simultaneously give ourselves to the good work of doing justice (that which is morally and ethically right), loving kindness (to see relationships thrive in mutual benevolence), and be humble before the Lord (be constantly aware that we are not God, but subject to his sovereign authority). This is good work! When Piper wrote to address the church during the Coronavirus pandemic, he gave instruction that sounds very similar to this charge in Micah, saying that "the good deeds of God's people will include prayers for the healing of the sick and for God to stay his hand and turn back the pandemic, and that he would provide a cure."[80]

We've already addressed the issue of trusting in God, but one final thought should be to obeying God. During our time of waiting, as we commune with the Lord and give ourselves to his work, we must expect that the Holy Spirit will direct us in more particular matters. Andrew Murray says that there is a certain degree of obedience which we learn from spending time in the Word consistently, but that "there is a special individual application of these commands—God's will concerning each of us personally, which only the Holy Spirit can teach. And He will not teach it, except to those who have taken the vow of obedience."[81]

What does true waiting on the Lord look like in the midst of a disruption? Waiting on the Lord to intervene in a troubled work environment? Waiting on the Lord to calm the disruption of a troubled household? How do we wait on the Lord when our emotions have been disrupted by a negative prognosis from the doctor? We draw nigh to the Lord, stay active in his work of justice, kindness, and humility, and be obedient to the still small voice of the Holy Spirit who begins to speak directly to areas of our lives. Why are we waiting? Why is the Spirit speaking? There is an end result to our waiting, being strengthened for more work that God has in store for us.[82] Remember, waiting has an effect – a renewed strength.

---

[80] Piper, *Coronavirus*, chapter 10, np.
[81] Andrew Murray, *The School of Obedience* (London: J. Nisbet & Co., 1898), 99.
[82] Andrew Murray, *Working for God!: A Sequel to Waiting on God!* (New York; Chicago; Toronto: Fleming H. Revell, 1901), 11.

A RENEWED STRENGTH: THE EFFECT OF WAITING

WILL GAIN NEW STRENGTH

There is a great difference between renew and refill, yet most often, refill is the concept that we think of when we read this passage. We assume that waiting on the Lord refuels us, it reboots our system; but that is not what the passage here in Isaiah is saying. The renewing of our strength is an exchange; it is trading our current strength for an altogether different strength that God has for us. What would be the benefit of an exchange over a refilling? The difference can be rather significant. Perhaps we might consider the common household battery.

In a 2019 New York Times article, an interesting comparison was made between the latest nickel-metal hydride (NiMH) rechargeable batteries, and the alkaline disposable ones.[83] While the writer had much to say about the rechargeable battery that was praiseworthy, the main point of the article was that there are some conditions where a rechargeable battery is not the power source of choice. What was ironic about the article was the conditions when a disposable battery is preferred, and the reason(s) why. According to this reporter, some of the average, under-appreciated devices (wall clocks, headlamps, bike lights), warning devices (smoke alarms), and emergency kits all prefer disposable batteries. In other words, when the power is low on these items, it is recommended that you not seek to re-fill their power, but replace. Why? Although the newer rechargeable batteries take longer to lose their power, and may even be more cost-effective over time, "a rechargeable battery may hang on at a lower voltage for slightly longer, resulting in unexpected behavior."[84] Imagine any of these listed items 'acting unexpectedly.' What catastrophe(s) might occur?

Of course, we are far more complex than AA batteries, but we can learn a valid lesson from them. Consider some of the average, unappreciated tasks that we 'lose strength' in doing; you know, the wall clock, head lamp type of work. What happens when we lose the powers of discernment and wisdom, and the 'warning lights' come on far too late, if at all. Imagine, in those emergency situations, where God really has need of us but we just don't have the juice! How often do we encounter people (pastors, spouses,

---

[83] https://www.nytimes.com/2019/06/06/smarter-living/wirecutter/are-rechargeable-batteries-better-than-alkaline.html.

[84] Same article referenced in fn. 84.

professionals, parents) suffering from burnouts, breakouts, and bailouts...unexpectedly? Could it be that we continuously rely on old strength for new assignments? The Lord does not seek to merely refill our strength, because doing so would stunt our spiritual growth. The writer of Hebrews addresses this problem in 5:12, insisting that there comes a time when our spiritual diet ought to change – there should be a maturing. Just as sure as we ought to move from 'milk to meat,' we ought to move from strength to strength.

Marshall Goldsmith published an amazing book for entrepreneurs, entitled, *What Got You Here Won't Get You There: How Successful People Become Even More Successful*. One of the most profound sentences in the book is that "beliefs that carried us *here* may be holding us back in our quest to go *there*."[85] The same premise could be used here, in the context of strength. The strength that it took to get you *to* the place you were in life before the disruption, may not be the same strength that it will take to get you *through* the disruption. Moreover, what God is able to do in and through you, having made it out of your disruption, may require a new strength altogether.

This strength exchange is something that we desperately need – especially in times of disruption. The psalmist attests to this in Psalm 84:5-8, where he states that the man whose strength comes from God is blessed. This blessedness comes with an experience; for though he goes through difficulty (passes through the Valley of Baca), it is to him a spring. There is even an early rain that covers this dry space, as he goes from *strength to strength*. When we are waiting on God, he offers a strength unlike that on which we currently rely. You don't have strength to forgive? That's ok! You've run out of strength to remain? He has a greater strength for you. You don't feel that you will be able to rebuild after this? Worry not, but wait on God, and God alone! He has a strength exchange program, with guaranteed results! I would imagine that a God who changes not would still say today as he did to the Apostle Paul, 'My strength is made perfect in (your) weakness' (2 Corinthians, 12:9).

---

[85] Marshall Goldsmith *What Got You Here Won't Get You There: How Successful People Become Even More Successful* (New York: Hachette Books, 2007), 17-18, Kindle Edition. Emphasis mine.

MOUNT, RUN, WALK: THE EVIDENCE OF WAITING

We understand what it means to wait on God; it is an active state of devotion, justice, love, and humility. Solitude may sometimes be necessary, but isolation is never the end-goal. We have a greater understanding of the benefit – a strength exchange. This means that I can be worn-out and waiting. That is ok, it is actually when God shows himself strong to those waiting on him. What we'd like to know is whether or not the waiting is working. Has the exchange taken place?

I have had long battles of weight management. I had what some laughingly have called the 'Luther Vandross Syndrome.' Luther was an R&B/Soul music singer whose weight seemed to change with the seasons (and for some reason, everyone's favorite was 'big Luther'). Every now and then, I'd hear about a new fat burner vitamin at the health store, and want to try it. Especially in my bigger days, there wasn't a price tag too high. What was most important to me was the evidence; how would I know if this B6, organic, twice harvested, picked from the top of mount whozawhat would actually work? What was the sign (other than waiting for the scale to move) that this was a good buy? If they offered no guarantee, I wasn't interested. The beauty of the passage currently in view is that God offers a guarantee here – a new strength *is indeed* the results of waiting on God, and this is how we will know that it is working...

THEY WILL MOUNT UP WITH WINGS LIKE EAGLES

The imagery of the eagle in the Bible should not be taken lightly. It was the chief bird of the air. The eagle soars in the heavens in obedience to the creation command of God. He instructed that birds "fly above the earth in the open expanse of the heavens" (Genesis 1:20). It is interesting that the eagle was able to perform, by design, what man tried to design through performance. Read Genesis 11. Far before NASA ever existed, before anyone took a step on the moon, much earlier than our fascination for Star Trek, Star Wars, and Dancing with the Stars, humanity has been trying to reach the heavens. While the eagle was created to naturally soar 'in the heavens,' mankind was trying to construct a tower that would reach the heavens. There was a great difference.

If we just looked at the book of Genesis, there is much to be stated about what is implied by mounting up with wings like eagles. God never had a problem with humans building. He was never intimidated by us building high. In fact, no matter how high we build, God will still have to 'come down' to see what we have made. He is, and forever will be 'higher' than we are (Isaiah 55:9). He is God. The problem in Genesis 11 was not their production, but the purpose in it. Genesis 11:4 says that they were not building in a way that would honor God; quite the opposite. They were building 'for their own name'. Even more, they wanted to build a great tower that could contain all of humanity that existed at the time, and they said, "otherwise we will be scattered abroad over the face of the whole earth." Here's the problem: the direct command from God was that humanity was *supposed* to 'scatter abroad over the face of the earth' (see Genesis 1:28). God was therefore not bothered by a tower; he was bothered by the resistance to 'fill the earth' as he had already commanded. Adam and Eve sinned by biting the fruit, and here humankind sins by building a mega-playpen. Here is the key – they were doing something within their capacity, but outside of God's command. That is a big deal!

This is what I believe it means to 'mount up on wings like eagles;' it is moving according to his *command* (that which God has said we must), into his allowed *capacity* (that which God has designed so that we can). The strength that God gives us is a strength that empowers us to dream, to imagine, and to try. It is the strength to start a business, although you don't come from a family of wealth or entrepreneurs. It is the strength to foster and adopt, when you cannot conceive. It is the strength to apply for college, even with a scathing academic history. It is the strength to write a book, though your last blog entry was two years ago when you graduated seminary. Simply put, this strength is not merely a strength to submit, it is a strength to soar; a strength to do that which is outside of your norm, but well within your God-given capacity. Waiting on God results in a strength that enables you to take up things that he has placed in your heart, but you hadn't the courage or the resources to take up, yet somehow, you 'take flight.'

That moment…you've experienced it, I am sure. The surreal moment where you look up and realize that the view is much different. You don't know how it happened; in fact, you wait for that instant where you wake up from it all and realize that it was just a dream. The strength that we gain from waiting on God places us wholly in that space. Not only is it a strength that moves us further toward our capacity, but it is a strength that enables us to see things and situations from a greater perspective; it is a strength that offers somewhat of a divine vantage point. One of the incredible features of an eagle is their impressively sharp vision and intense speed. From great distances, they can spot their prey, and move in swiftly to take them by surprise.[86] Oftentimes when we are facing a disruption, perspective is one of the least of our concerns; yet as we will see in a later chapter, it is one of the greatest things that we covet. From an eagle's elevation, I can see beyond the immediate. I can see what I need for sustenance. I can see where I might find rest. I can watch over those in my care. Perspective can change the entire outcome of a disruption.

A final word on the eagle is the path of least resistance. It is a word of hope for those who are in the midst of a difficult season and feel like every move they make is met by obstacles. God promises to give a strength that mounts his people up on wings like eagles. Such a position puts them on a trajectory that is void of natural obstacles. No longer slowed down by the trees, the impassable waters, nor the mountains. In fact, mounting up on wings as eagles may be the realization of such prayers of faith that says to the mountain 'be thou removed, and be cast into the sea' (Mark 11:23). It may just be that the elevation of the mountain range which once occupied the horizon, is now brought as low as the sea as a result of our soaring.

THEY WILL RUN AND NOT GET TIRED

As exciting as it may be to know that God grants us a strength that enables us to dream bigger, see further, and move with more freedom, there is also the reality of natural tasks. Even the eagle cannot stay in the air forever. There is work that must be done 'on the ground.' Dreams and passions do not cancel out demands and priorities. Running should not be understood here as merely accelerated footwork, but more clearly the act of being busy.[87] Understanding this distinction has incredible implications for the one who is waiting on God, but life isn't slowing down. The strength described here is akin to an adrenaline rush. It promises that the strength of God empowers us to move at the pace of life, without suffering physical or emotional exhaustion.[88]

Such a claim may make some feel a little uncomfortable; to suggest that waiting on God makes sleepiness and fatigue go away, or physical

---

[86] Allen C. Myers, *The Eerdmans Bible Dictionary* (Grand Rapids, MI: Eerdmans, 1987), 297.

[87] רוּץ, *NIDOTTE*, 1084.

[88] יָגֵעַ, *NIDOTTE*, 400. "the vb. denotes be/become tired, physically and/or emotionally exhausted."

strength defy human limits. First, even if this is my claim (though it is not), it does not move beyond the realm of true faith in God. The creator of humanity created humanity with limits. I would like to press the issue a little further, on a practical note. For a moment, let us think back to what true waiting on God is – trust and obedience.

One of our most difficult areas of obedience is that of observing the sabbath (Exodus 20:8-11). While this is a topic that has been gravely misunderstood, mistaught, and mismanaged, the command is nevertheless from God to *all* of his special creation – humankind. The command to remember the sabbath is not about a day of the week – it's about a day *in* the week; meaning, it is about taking a day, any day, to rest. The problem is what Curtis Zuckery calls "this-world" thinking. He describes the issue quite well:

> As human beings, we have an adversarial relationship with time. When we are young, it seems that time cannot move fast enough. We want to be older; we want to get out on our own; we want to be able to do our own thing. Once we reach a certain point, we begin to desire for time to slow down… When we practice the Sabbath and intentionally move away from the regular rhythms that come from our work and accomplishments, we cease to be bound by "this-world" thinking… Our focus shifts to the worship and acknowledgment of the God, who has made this world and held it in His hand. The toil and strain we are subjected to as a result of the work of our hand are put to the side and supplanted by the refreshment that comes with acknowledging God.[89]

While running and not getting tired may sound quite supernatural and other-worldly, it might just be the most natural thing that we can experience when living in full obedience to God. Perhaps such a strength is a natural result of obedient rest. When we rest from our work, it is an act of worship and gratitude. Would God not reward this type of obedience with a new strength for the work to which we will return?

---

[89] Curtis Zackery, *Soul Rest: Reclaim Your Life; Return to Sabbath*, ed. Abigail Stocker et al. (Bellingham, WA: Kirkdale Press, 2018), 49.

Life is busy. Whether you are single, married, wealthy or unemployed; life is busy! The unfortunate reality of disruptions is that they don't slow life down, they seem to speed it up. When the Coronavirus Pandemic hit the state of Michigan in late March, 2020, schools closed, businesses shut down, churches adapted to online streaming, and many corporate employees learned what it meant to 'work from home.' We could no longer freely shop at the local grocery store without a care. Gloves, masks, and hand sanitizer were the new keys, purse, and wallet – don't leave home without them. While it might seem that a society that is shut down and sheltered in place would be less busy, quite the opposite was true for most people, if not for everyone. That is just the way disruptions work – they enhance the busy. We find ourselves doing more and sleeping less. What God promises is that when we wait (trust and obey... including rest) on him, we will not become victims of this 'enhanced busy.'

THEY WILL WALK AND NOT BECOME WEARY

Finally, the promise is to walk without the thought of giving up. The context(s) of running and walking may not necessarily be different, but the conditions may be very different. Parenting can have its busy seasons. Then there are seasons that almost feel like you are running on auto-pilot. If you have a full quiver like Karen and I, that auto-pilot feature does not come on often enough. Certainly God knows that we need strength, not only to dream, and not just to make it through our busy seasons, but making it day to day takes a fresh strength as well. Warren Weirsbe explains how important this strength is:

> It is much harder to walk in the ordinary pressures of life than to fly like the eagle in a time of crisis...The greatest heroes of faith are not always those who seem to be soaring; often it is they who are patiently plodding. As we wait on the Lord, He enables us not only to fly higher and run faster, but also *to walk longer*. Blessed are the plodders, for they eventually arrive at their destination![90]

Strength for the long haul: this is what God promises to us – strength to go the distance. It is the strength to hold on even when God seems to be holding out. Walking strength is the type that you need when the results

---

[90] Warren W. Wiersbe, *Be Comforted*, "Be" Commentary Series (Wheaton, IL: Victor Books, 1996), 112.

don't seem to be coming as fast as you desire. It is the strength to save money when alluring advertisements continue to bombard your social media feed and inbox. It is the strength to meal-prep for another week when the scale seems not to budge. These things may seem trivial in a discussion about disruptions, but are they really?

How often do the disruptions of life cause us to forget the small things, the unhurried things? Disruptions break traditions, cancel plans, stifle good practices. If God created us to do *good works*, would things like date night, weight loss, family-time, or even finishing a good book not be something that he desires of us? Yet it is often these simple things that we fail to seek strength from God to maintain. We want them, we envy them, and even when we do talk to God about them, our motives are skewed (James 4:1-3). So, the promise here of walking strength ensures that we do not have to simply wish, envy, and quarrel; but to wait on God.

How do we know that our feeble strength has been exchanged for a strength from God? We can be in the midst of a disruption yet have a vision beyond the current circumstances. Perhaps we see that which God has created us with the capacity (passion and persistence) to do. More than perceive it, we feel empowered to actually pursue it. The evidence is also in our ability to navigate the busy seasons without feeling overwhelmed; it is seen in our trusted resting *in* him, and returning to work refreshed *by* him. And finally, when we see ourselves strengthened to stay the course in the simplest things, the unhurried things, then we know – an exchange has been made!

WHAT ARE YOU WAITING FOR?

Waiting is not a question. You are waiting. You will wait. The question is, what will you be waiting for? Just as sure as we breathe, we will face disruptions. No one knows how long our disruptions will last – we only know that they come. The object of our waiting will determine the outcome of our disruption. If we choose to wait on anything other than God, no matter how promising that substitute might be, the outcome is simply delay! There is no inherent danger in delays. In fact, our culture has discovered ways to make delays entertaining. From social media, to short-run streaming services like Quibi,[91] we have found ways to 'fill the time' of delay. But when it comes to the plan and purpose of God for our lives, delay can be a very dangerous thing. The wise teacher writing in Ecclesiastes 5 says that unnecessary delay, as it relates to the things we do for God, is foolish and something God takes no delight in (Ecclesiastes 5:1-9).

What came of my laid-off waiting season? I learned how to wait. Not for an apology, not for a new work assignment, not for an opportunity to share my story; I waited on God. That was the year that I began writing in a journal. I did not pray long prayers, or even consistent prayers before that, but I loved to write. I used my journal as a way to talk to God. Instead of talking to God, I wrote him letters every day. I waited…I trusted and obeyed. I drew closer to God, and tried to live a life that reflected that closeness. I hadn't even realized the change, but I had a new strength that I would never have imagined. I started a business, purchased a home, and provided for my family even better than I did when I worked as a contractor. God even used this time to open a door for me to enter vocational ministry (the job training director position mentioned earlier). Although I still had a lesson to learn on *working* for God at the time (as discussed before), in this situation I did learn a lesson in *waiting* on God! I soared, I ran, and I walked, and the outcome of that disruption set me on a new trajectory.

Friend, I encourage you – do not let this end in delay. You might feel like you are losing time, but you were created by a God who exists outside of time. It is not you who causes things to work together for good, but the timeless God whom you serve (Romans 8:28). His ways are not our ways, nor his thoughts our thoughts, they are unimaginably greater (Isaiah 55:8-9). Disruptions are a necessary part of life (Ecclesiastes 3:1-10), but they do have an expiration date. No matter what your disruption is – you will come out of it. Will you come out matured? Wiser? More focused? Or will you come out of this right where you started? It all depends. *What are you waiting for?*

---

[91] Quibi was a short-lived streaming service that emerged in 2019 and dismantled in 2020. Their niche was providing short-run original series with episodes only lasting seven to ten minutes. The idea was that subscribers could enjoy entertainment while waiting in grocery lines, waiting rooms, barber shops, etc.

QUESTIONS FOR REFLECTION

1. In this chapter, I offered a chart of authority. Take a moment and think of 1 or 2 **DISRUPTIONS** wherein you found yourself waiting. Create a similar chart of your own. What was the **DISRUPTION** (scenario)? Who or what did you give authority to (what were you waiting for)? On what basis? Can you recognize the problem in this waiting scenario?

2. I offer several Old Testament passages of Scripture that give examples of waiting on God; however, waiting on God is not simply an Old Testament topic. Read Paul's argument for waiting in Romans 8:18-25. Explain how this passage is helpful instruction for those facing a **DISRUPTION**.

3. If waiting can be defined as 'active trust' in God, what do you find most challenging about waiting on God when facing a **DISRUPTION**?

4. In a few brief sentences, write a 'declaration of active trust' for yourself. What does this mean to you, specifically? What will you cease from doing? What will you commit to actively doing?

5. We conclude this chapter with the question, 'What are you waiting for?'. Does the exploration of Isaiah 40:31 cause you to reconsider how you wait on the Lord in your **DISRUPTIONS**? How so?

4 DEATH: WHAT ARE YOU SAYING?

When we talk about delays, we are talking about losing time. But there are some disruptions that impact us in such a way that more than *time* is lost. Sometimes, it is our purpose, our dreams, our plans, or our motivation that is lost. We experience it all the time; disruptions that lead to death. Name five people closest to you, and I will name *at least* four who have personally experienced a disruption that led to death. One of the effects of the COVID-19 pandemic was that some businesses had to close. Social distancing and shelter-in-place orders meant that some small businesses would no longer be able to service their customers until these orders were lifted.

As time passed, the thought of even resuming business became a fairy tale for many. Some walked away from leases, contract negotiations, some from their trade altogether. Some pastors stopped preaching to their congregations. They did not feel as though they could adapt to the new norm of streaming online. Nonprofits ceased and desisted in serving their communities, as resources began to dissipate. If you remember, this book draws on lessons from the Coronavirus Pandemic, but it is not a memoir of the events. Think about some disruptions that you have experienced, or have been affected by, that have led to death.

Perhaps this might be an important place to pause and address the fact that death itself can be a disruption. Certainly, there are those who have lost a loved one, and it tore their world apart. As a minister in the inner-city, I have either officiated or attended too many funerals of young people who were fatal victims of crime. Most of these young people were innocent bystanders, but some of them were unfortunately entangled in criminal activity. Guilty or innocent, their deaths ripped holes in the fabric of their households; especially those whose families were not Christian, and gave no thought to one day seeing their loved one again in heaven. While the t-shirts, and urban memorial shrines might speak of angels getting wings, and resting in heaven, there was no real sense of life after death. This event called death is indeed a disruption.

It doesn't have to be the death of a young child falling victim to senseless crime; it could be the loss of a spouse, a parent, a close friend. It could be a death of natural causes, suicide, an accident, or it could be a miscarriage. Regardless of the individual or the circumstances, it is necessary that we acknowledge the fact that death can be a disruption in and of itself. One of the realities of the Coronavirus disruption is that it has not only led to figurative death, but there is a true death toll that was climbing daily. While death can be a disruption in and of itself, we still need to look at the non-physical death that disruptions can lead to. Let us remember, however, that it is not the disruption itself that leads to a figurative death. It is our activity amid the disruption that determines this type of outcome.

I remember the summer of 2017 like it was just a few months ago. I will probably never get the eerie smell and grey scene out of my mind. It was just before 5am, and the sun had not yet kissed the sky of our street corner. The solar-powered streetlamp on the corner was coming to the end of its charge. There I stood, in front of my home, scared, tearful, and full of questions. Wait on God…I got that. Learned that lesson; but the severity of this disruption is much greater than being laid off – we're talking funeral type of disruptions here.

It was mid-June, and I was taking a modular class on campus at Moody Theological Seminary in Chicago, nearing the end of my degree. Since it was a week-long class, I thought it would be good to have my family there with me, and we'd hang out in the city after class. The second night there, I received a call from my younger sister who was housesitting. "Hello!!! Aaron!?" she said, frantically, "Ummm…I think the house is on fire!" Thinking that she was perhaps being a little overdramatic, or burned something by accident, I began to ask questions… you know, the typical – where are you? Is anyone hurt? Where's the fire? At the time of the call, she had made it outside. The house was indeed on fire. An electrical fire had started in the basement, beneath the kitchen – right near the electrical box. It took out the electricity of the entire house! The fire erupted beneath our newly remodeled kitchen – burning a hole in the center of the floor. Having no power in the house, the fire department had to come through whatever window they found. Imagine the sight, having nearly thirty windows in the house.

So there I was – after four and a half hours of racing from Chicago to Detroit, standing and smelling my charred, dark, unwelcoming home. I walked in through the broken door, over the broken glass. I had Karen and the kids stay in the car, because I didn't want them to see the fear that had overtaken me. I heard the dripping of the water that had rushed through the fire hoses not too long before. The first responders tried their best to salvage my home. There was not much fire damage beyond the kitchen and the inside walls, but the smoke damage was severe. You could see it everywhere.

Curtains – damaged. Bedding – done. Clothes – ruined. My books... Lord, help me!

The scene was so sad. I was at least confident that our homeowner's insurance would cover the damage, but, among other issues with our policy, we found out that our insurance did not cover electric fires for historic homes, such as ours. ***DISRUPTION!***

I tried to hide my emotions. I took my family to my sister-in-law's home, and told my wife that I would take care of everything – do not worry! I slept for a few hours, and went to the house later that morning. I had a plan. I would board the windows, get a storage unit to put all of our expensive salvageable things in, and wait...that was all I could think of. I walked into the house, stood in the foyer, and looked around. By this time, my mom and my sister came to the house, to encourage, and help. It didn't matter. I stood in the dining room, and broke down weeping. "It's over!" I had been in this home for ten years. We had plans for the house. We had money saved up, but that money was earmarked for future things, not rehabbing a home! We didn't even have enough to hire contractors to do the work. IT. IS. OVER! ***DISRUPTION!!***

I thought it. I said it. And I walked out of the house with the weight of it on my shoulders. Where would we live now? All of our savings would have to go to purchasing a new home – but we'd NEVER be able to find something like what we have now, based on what we have saved. Hello downsizing. Of course, I'd have to drop out of seminary. In fact, I should email my professors and let them know now... and I did! Why stop at the kitchen, God?! Shoot! Why not just take the whole thing!? Nothing that I can do anyway. ***DISRUPTION!!!***

Perhaps you can relate to a similar situation where your diagnosis was simply, IT IS OVER! You were facing a disruption that was simply insurmountable. I will share with you the lesson that I learned from this, but first we should look to Scripture and witness the experience of two sisters who faced a disruption that led to death. These two sisters did what I did, and what many of us do in the midst of a disruption: they became preachers and pallbearers. Preachers are the one who offer the eulogy at a funeral. Pallbearers are the ones who carry the 'dead weight.' Unfortunately, disruptions cause us to do both – we consider things as dead, then carry the weight of our eulogy that we have preached. Let's look at Mary and Martha as a case study.

OH BROTHER, THIS IS BAD!

> **John 11:1–46 (NASB)**
>
> ¹ Now a certain man was sick, Lazarus of Bethany, the village of Mary and her sister Martha. ² It was the Mary who anointed the Lord with ointment, and wiped His feet with her hair, whose brother Lazarus was sick. ³ So the sisters sent word to Him, saying, "Lord, behold, he whom You love is sick."

This disruption is not a reflection of broken communion with God. We visited this earlier in the second chapter, but it is worth noting and revisiting here. John makes it very clear. Lazarus was not sick because he was at odds with Jesus. Much more, he wasn't just a man whom Jesus was familiar with, or even fond of – Lazarus was 'he whom you love.' Yet, devotion does not make us exempt from disruptions. As we will soon see, this was no mere annoyance, such as a common cold, or even a flu virus. Lazarus was dying.

> ⁴ But when Jesus heard this, He said, "This sickness is not to end in death, but for the glory of God, so that the Son of God may be glorified by it."

Hmmm. Perhaps it is a matter of semantics if someone tried to call Jesus out on this, but he said that it doesn't end in death. If you know the story, you are already ahead of me. Spoiler alert…Lazarus dies. I need to make sure that we are all aware of that before moving on, because it has significant implications. Jesus did not say that Lazarus would not die. Read it carefully; what he is saying is actually *better!* Even in a worst-case scenario... death does not mean done! This disruption doesn't end in weeping, but in worship. I believe this is certainly true for our disruptions. Which brings God more glory? Life would have been great if this had never happened, but since it had happened, now God can show his greatness.

> ⁵ Now Jesus loved Martha and her sister and Lazarus. ⁶ So when He heard that he was sick, He then stayed two days longer in the place where He was. ⁷ Then after this He said to the disciples, "Let us go to Judea again."

We might call this the 'flag on the play.' Jesus hears that Lazarus is facing a disruption, yet seems to make no effort to get there? And notice the affirmation once more. Jesus is not delaying for the sake of discipline or reprimand. Their relationship is not in question. Sometimes God will simply allow the disruption to take its course. He was fully aware of the circumstances, even the severity, but he waited. Just as he could have prevented the fire in my house or prevented the supervisor from offering slanderous testimony that cost me my job. Sometimes for his own reasons – namely, his own glory, God allows bad to get worse.

> [8] The disciples said to Him, "Rabbi, the Jews were just now seeking to stone You, and are You going there again?" [9] Jesus answered, "Are there not twelve hours in the day? If anyone walks in the day, he does not stumble, because he sees the light of this world. [10] "But if anyone walks in the night, he stumbles, because the light is not in him." [11] This He said, and after that He said to them, "Our friend Lazarus has fallen asleep; but I go, so that I may awaken him out of sleep."

Lazarus is asleep?! Is that your assessment, Jesus? How often do we forget that God's perspective of our disruption is so much greater than our own? Two comforting and convicting points are being affirmed by Jesus; Lazarus is precious, and Lazarus has a purpose! 'Our friend' is sleeping, Jesus says; but it is a sleep that Jesus must wake him from. It is comforting to know that in our disruptions, we still have value (remember the twenty-dollar bill bit). But it is convicting to think of how many other things we expect to 'awaken' us. Standing in front of my singed home, I was looking for my insurance company to awaken me. Although I had a host of thoughts flood my mind, none of them were 'I am precious to God…he has plans for me beyond this!'

> [12] The disciples then said to Him, "Lord, if he has fallen asleep, he will recover." [13] Now Jesus had spoken of his death, but they thought that He was speaking of literal sleep. [14] So Jesus then said to them plainly, "Lazarus is dead, [15] and I am glad for your sakes that I was not there, so that you may believe; but let us go to him." [16] Therefore

> Thomas, who is called Didymus, said to his fellow disciples, "Let us also go, so that we may die with Him."

Here is a great lesson to learn; the delayed intervention is for our benefit. We find this truth taught in James 1, but here we witness it in the laboratory of life. It's like Jesus is saying... "If I showed up when you wanted...every time you faced a disruption, your faith would never grow to know that I am God even when things are as bad as they can possibly be!"

> [17] So when Jesus came, He found that he had already been in the tomb four days. [18] Now Bethany was near Jerusalem, about two miles off; [19] and many of the Jews had come to Martha and Mary, to console them concerning their brother.

Verse 17 is a very sobering part of this story. Here is where things don't really add up, on the surface. "Love" and "this sickness is not to end in death" do not equal a four-day tomb stay. Yet, when Jesus arrives, this is the state in which Lazarus is found. We must remember, Jesus did not say that the sickness would not *lead to* death, only that it wouldn't *end in* death. Our problem is that we often overestimate our understanding of our purpose and his process. The two are far beyond our comprehension when it comes to God. God is omnipresent; he exists outside of time and space, so his care and capacity are not restricted by our present circumstance(s) – even if our felt reality says that it is over. No matter how much we ponder it, we would never understand the depths of love and concern that God has for us. The unselfish act of his suffering at Calvary is enough to remind us that he is concerned.

> [20] Martha therefore, when she heard that Jesus was coming, went to meet Him, but Mary stayed at the house. [21] Martha then said to Jesus, "Lord, if You had been here, my brother would not have died.

Martha is out, Mary is in. It is interesting how disruptions can turn spiritual devotion into social distancing. Notice how this disruption flips the storyline. In Luke 10:38-42, we see that Mary was the one running out to Jesus, worshipping at his feet. Now, she won't even come out of the house.

Have you ever had a disruption eat away at your devotion? No more foot washing, Mary is weeping.

> [22] "Even now I know that whatever You ask of God, God will give You." [23] Jesus said to her, "Your brother will rise again." [24] Martha said to Him, "I know that he will rise again in the resurrection on the last day." [25] Jesus said to her, "I am the resurrection and the life; he who believes in Me will live even if he dies, [26] and everyone who lives and believes in Me will never die. Do you believe this?" [27] She said to Him, "Yes, Lord; I have believed that You are the Christ, the Son of God, even He who comes into the world."

While Martha may have missed it in Luke's gospel account, she certainly makes up for it here. Martha has what I call an 'eschatological affirmation' (she looks, with hope, to life beyond death), but what she is looking for is hope *in the midst of* disruption! We can relate to her position. We don't want to know that there is a light at the end of the tunnel; we want to know that there is a door, mid-way that leads to a staircase to the surface! What Martha is struggling with here is faith and facts. Her faith says that she knows that Jesus could heal (he had a track record of it). The fact is that he wasn't there. Her faith says that there is a resurrection of the body in the future; this was an accepted Jewish reality. The fact is that she did not expect to lose her brother this soon; she doesn't want to wait till 'that great day.' Jesus responds with the great fact on which all faith rests; HE is the resurrection...not *what will be* - but *what is right now*!

Here is a good time to momentarily break away from the text, and unpack this story in the context of our own disruptions. How is it that Lazarus had already gone through the process of a funeral service and a burial? It was because of the preachers and the pallbearers.

PREACHERS & PALLBEARERS

As I stated earlier, when we face disruptions, we sometimes take on the role of preachers and pallbearers. How do we know if we are in danger of becoming either? Let's look at each role individually, and their implications on the outcome of our disruptions. Our role of the preacher is evidenced in the words that we say; our complaints and conversations. We must not restrict these words to the audible expressions that come from our mouth. Our social media speaks for us; a picture is worth a thousand words, and a video is a whole lot of pictures! Our actions speak *louder* than our words. We embody the pallbearer by the weight that we carry: mental and emotional weights that we have, only because we have eulogized that which has seemingly ended in death.

THE ART OF PREACHING

I am sure that you have heard preaching before; good preaching…bad preaching…you've heard it. Whether you've heard preaching before or not, it is not enough to say that disruptions turn us into preachers. I must explore this thing called preaching so that we all have a more informed idea of just how serious of an impact this role has. Preaching is an art; a diverse and complex craft where study, substance, situation, and style all converge. In a way, one could argue that everyone is a preacher – though not everyone is preaching the same sermon. Since this is not a book on preaching, the discussion here will be brief. In my library, I have shelves that are dedicated wholly to the art of preaching – black preaching, topical preaching, narrative preaching, preaching to kids, preaching to crowds, *Real Preachers of LA*... Instead of trying to cover or even introduce various styles, I will focus on just a few principles that govern the development and delivery of a well-crafted sermon.

I am not sure if there is a Bible School or seminary teaching a course on homiletics (preaching) which does not at least reference the late Haddon Robinson (no relation, although I wouldn't miss a family reunion if we were!). A former homiletics professor in various universities and president of Denver Seminary, to say that Robinson was an expert on preaching would be an understatement. One major contribution that he made to the art and craft of a sermon was the Big Idea. Robinson taught that a sermon should have a 'Big Idea,' one central thought that governed the sermon. He was convinced that "sermons seldom fail because they have too many ideas; more often they fail because they deal with too many unrelated ideas."[92] When I studied at Moody, Dr. Tucker, would require us to state our Big Idea five to seven times in a sermon.

---

[92] Haddon Robinson, *Biblical Preaching: The Development and Delivery of Expository Messages* (Grand Rapids, MI: Baker Publishing Group, 1980), 49.

Formulating the big idea is not always easy, although we are quite familiar with the concept. Outside of a church context, the big idea concept is certainly memorable in the political arena. Whether you were wholeheartedly convinced, "Yes We Can!" or you were passionately committed to "Make America Great Again!" you rallied behind a well communicated 'Big Idea'! This is not an endorsement of a political stance; it is an endorsement of a communication standard. In his book, *Biblical Preaching*, Robinson explains how the big idea is developed; one must have both a subject and a complement.[93] The subject is the thing that you are talking about, and the complement is what you are saying about that thing. While this might seem simple enough to understand, it goes a little deeper than this. Bear with me just a little more – I know you didn't sign up for a preaching class, but you will soon see how disruptions put you in the school of preaching, whether you like it or not.

To best understand the big idea in practice, let's look again at the narrative in John. While neither Mary nor Martha probably considered themselves preachers, they certainly had a well-thought-out big idea! In verse 21, Martha says to Jesus, "If you had been here, my brother would not have died." Those are weighty words! This was her 'Yes We Can!'; it was her 'MAGA!'. In verse 32, we recognize it as a big idea, because Mary comes and echoes, "Lord, if You had been here, my brother would not have died." Surely, these sisters must have had time to talk over the past several days – perhaps even days before. Remember, Lazarus was *in the tomb* four days. This means that there was a sickness period, a death, a period of anointing and preparing the body for burial (a Jewish custom), a funeral, then placing him in the tomb. Significant time for conversation.

Remember, a big idea must have a subject (what am I talking about), and a complement (what am I saying about what I am talking about). Let's reverse engineer Mary's and Martha's big idea, and discover the subject and compliment of their sermon.

---

[93] See 'The Formation of an Idea' in Robinson, *Biblical Preaching,* 60-62.

> **BIG IDEA:** Lord, if You had been here, my brother would not have died.
>
> **SUBJECT:** Our brother, Lazarus was gravely ill.
>
> **COMPLEMENT:** Because Jesus, who is well known for his healing power, was not present when things were merely uncomfortable, the illness evolved to the point of fatality, causing us to lose someone very dear to us.

Can you see how these two realities (subject and complement) work together to create one memorable idea that can be communicated with ease of repetition? And so, we have our big idea to begin preaching our sermon. The big idea is not the sermon itself, but it is the vehicle which carries the sermon. Now, the challenge before us is to take this big idea, and create a homiletic masterpiece.

PREACHING WITH WORDS

This masterpiece which we seek to construct is multi-sensory. This theory is proven by the booming multi-media industry that exists within the church: lights, screens, sounds, etc. No matter how creative and multi-sensory you get, preaching will still involve words – words written, spoken, read, sang, illustrated, or performed. Unfortunately, the choice of words is not often intentional and well-thought-out for the preacher who has a disruption as their homiletics professor. Many times, faith, fact, and fear converge in our sermons. We affirm that we believe God can – that he is ultimately in control. Yet, while there is faith in our words, there is a degree of painful fact that we cannot seem to let escape our speech. The facts cause fear to set in our mind, resulting in a sermon of lament: 'This situation hurts!' In fact, the pain is often very directed; 'This situation, *which you allowed,* hurts!'

When we are in a disruption, we have many preaching outlets. Just as the Spirit cries out in the book of Revelation, "He who has ears to hear, let him listen!" so does our hurt and pain cry out in our disruption! We long for an audience. Even in our seasons of isolation, many of us are longing to be missed from the crowd; hoping for a phone call or a text, 'What's wrong?' so that we will have a chance to preach our sermon from the disruption – even if our sermon dismisses their attempts. Although I know there are exceptions to this claim, the situation is not uncommon. We preach sermons in our casual conversations, in our social media feeds, even in our choice of music and entertainment, all roads for our big idea. Have you noticed when you are going through a personal disruption, how that 'big idea' would find its way into conversation after conversation? No one would ask you, but it would come up somehow! Perhaps you didn't notice it, but someone else did and pointed it out. Congratulations… you're a preacher!

PREACHING WITH ILLUSTRATION

While many might argue (and many biblical scholars have) that Martha is saying good, faithful things here, let us not forget that preaching is multi-sensory. Martha's sermon began well before Jesus arrived. She had been preaching what we would call an 'illustrated sermon.' Think of sermons that are performance based. Pastors often do this around Christmas and Easter. Illustrated sermons can often be sermons of the most powerful type.

Generally, the illustrated sermon involves people, props, and even places. These sorts of sermons "embody the [big idea] in a concrete way, but do this by means of a full-fledged story, with a beginning, middle and end…" and "they show us someone acting on the principle."[94] For Mary and Martha, there was a sermon being preached with every invitation of a mourner to their home. Every oil and fragrance they prepared for the anointing and burial was another point in their sermon. The body was buried and the house was full. While their conviction was that Jesus could, their choreography (arrangement of movements) was that Jesus wouldn't. If he cared enough, he would have gotten here and stopped this in its early stages. They had all the people (weeping mourners), props (fragrances, oils, burial linen), and places (tomb and back home for the repast) for the making of a great illustrated sermon.

Big idea: If Jesus had been here, Lazarus would not have died.

Consider the people that we employ in the drama of our illustrated sermons. Spouses, children, friends – all play an active role. Perhaps it is co-workers or church members who have a part in the performance. Our props vary in size and shape. Alcohol, pornography, money, drugs, work, time; the list is endless. Just as endless is the list of places that provide the scenes of

---

[94] David Heywood, *Transforming Preaching: The Sermon as a Channel for God's Word*, SPCK Library of Ministry (London: SPCK, 2013), 104.

our illustrated sermons: even the playground of our mind is a scene. We employ who we can, what we can, and where we can, in order to get the big idea across....

If God had shown up, _____ would not have happened!

PREACHING WITH EXPECTATION

One more thing about sermons; preachers don't preach just to hear themselves speak – although admittedly sometimes, it does sound like we do... myself included. Ultimately, the purpose of preaching is transformation.[95] Through sermons, we seek to form ideals, as well as identities. Our aim as preachers is to help people live with a particular conviction of 'this is who I am to be.' Sermons have a 'so what?' factor to them. As Robinson argues, "a sermon touches life. It demands practical application."[96] Again, let's not relegate the sermon to the pulpit of the church, but think beyond the walls of the congregations into more public spheres. What was the practical application of President Obama's sermons centering around the big idea 'Yes We Can!'? What practical application would President Trump's sermons incite to manifest the big idea, 'Make America Great Again!'? It is not just politics. Allstate Insurance Company presents many illustrated sermons in the form of television commercials by preaching their big idea, 'You're in good hands!'. Nike invokes the aid of many celebrities and athletes to help preach the big idea, 'Just Do It!'. In all of these things, there is an intended action! Whether we want people to vote, shop, try, or live life differently, sermons require action.

The case is no different for Mary and Martha in their disruption. Every character in this unfolding drama was acting on expectation. Whether they expected Jesus to arrive, his disciples to accompany him, many people to show up and mourn with them, people to help anoint, wrap, and bury...everyone had a role to play. When we preach, we point people in a particular direction. The moment that Lazarus's illness took a fatal turn, Martha and Mary began pointing people in a specific direction with their big idea: Jesus wasn't here, therefore all we can do is mourn and bury. While we can commend Martha's faith in telling Jesus 'Even now, I know that

---

[95] Heywood, *Transforming Preaching*, 16.
[96] Haddon Robinson, "Chapter Four: Blending Bible Content and Life Application," in *Mastering Contemporary Preaching* (Portland, OR: Multnomah, 1989), 59.

anything you ask of God, God will give you.' it is not the conviction in the sermon that she preached when they anointed and buried Lazarus. If that were the case, Lazarus's body would have been lying in a room in the house and the people there would not have been mourning, but praying, waiting to witness a miracle.

Are you convinced that we preach in our disruptions? Perhaps I can recap in a concise sentence. When a subject (the situation that concerns us) and a complement (what we have to say about that situation) converge to a big idea (one driving point), and that big idea is communicated, whether by word or illustration, with the expectancy that the listeners will act, you have a sermon. Proof that we preach sermons when we face disruptions can be seen in our social media feeds, papers that we have filed with the court, a quick glance at our bank statements, our internet browsing history, and more. We expect the hearers of our sermons to respond. Whether that response be signing divorce papers, liking a post, satisfying our need for attention, or countless other responses, we are preaching to be heard. What is our big idea? My marriage is over because God allowed _____. I will never own a business because God didn't _____. The problem with the sermon that we preach is that when it is a eulogy (sermon preached at a funeral), one of the expected responses is that pallbearers will come and carry the casket.

A BOX AND A BODY

The role of the pallbearer varies in different social contexts. It is actually quite interesting to observe the differences. Did you know that there are professional pallbearers!? I had no idea. In most of the funerals that I have participated in, the pallbearers have just been close friends and family members. But as my pastoral role expanded, I was introduced to funerals where professional pallbearers were hired for the funeral. The pageantry was absolutely intriguing to me. I was amazed and amused at the same time. I was amused, perhaps a little tickled at the fact that there was a rehearsed choreography to the whole event. I was amazed at the story that the choreography told. I'll never forget the funeral of a precious grandmother where a professional pallbearer team was employed. They played the organ and sang the old hymn, '…I'm going to put on my robe, tell my story, how I made it over.' Tears filled my eyes as they marched in perfect unison down the aisle, adorned the grandmother with a crown, and closed the casket. It was dramatic, it was unexpected, it was beautiful. But at the end of the day…in all reality…it was just a box and a body.

We expect people to carry the weight of our eulogies that we preach in the midst of our disruptions. The chief of these pallbearers is ourselves. No matter how creative the roles these pallbearers are asked to play, they are still just carrying dead weight. There are two elements of the pallbearer that I would like us to consider briefly before moving on. It is important that we consider the community of pallbearers as well as the cadence, or *rhythm of movement* of the pallbearers. Without intention, we can develop such a community, and such a cadence, that it takes our attention off the fact that this funeral shouldn't even be taking place.

THE PALLBEARER COMMUNITY

Who is carrying this weight with you? In a typical American funeral, you might find six or more pallbearers. Some cultures could have a dozen or more. The simple point is that pallbearing is not a solo task. In our disruptions, we invite loved ones. 'Come and carry this with me!' Sadly, we present it as if we have given them a place of honor in our lives. These weights that people are invited to carry are unnecessary weights. Friends are invited to carry the weight of broken dreams. Children are invited to carry the weight of divorce. Families and employees are invited to carry the weight of failed businesses. Congregations are invited to carry the weight of a pastoral resignation.

The community of pallbearers can be quite large. The problem lies in the comfort that they bring and the weight that they carry. For us, it is a load off; we have found someone(s) on whom we can cast our cares. We can vent, lash out, criticize, complain, and altogether lean on our pallbearers. For them, there is a heavy, unspoken sense of obligation, and a burden that they now must unfairly bear. I have witnessed some funerals where sixteen or more pallbearers served; six carrying the casket, and the others walked immediately behind. In a disruption, the community is similar. The rhythm of movement, to which we now turn, is also just as syncopated.

THE PALLBEARER CADENCE

You've seen it, I am sure: the militaristic march of focused individuals at the end of the funeral, carrying the casket from the front of the room to the hearse. That walk…that long, rhythmic, focused, walk: left, right, left, right, turn all together. That is the cadence. We may not realize it, but when we invite people to serve as pallbearers, we are asking them to commit to a specific walk, at a specific pace, for a designated amount of time. To be clear, that time does not expire until the casket goes in the ground. As pallbearers, they are required to join the ceremony until the ceremony is complete. Some funerals are designed such that even the seating arrangement of the pallbearers is pre-determined. How does this look in the funeral of disruption?

Far from honoring them, asking people to serve as pallbearers in our funeral of disruption is one of the most selfish acts imaginable. And who are we kidding? We don't ask. We demand and manipulate. If they really loved us, they would be more than willing to carry this weight with us. And by demanding that they carry this weight with us, we subsequently restrict their movement. Now they must follow our cadence until this thing is buried. Is this not true? I was offended, so this relationship is dead. As my pallbearer, I expect you to carry this dead relationship with me. When we talk, we need to talk about how they wronged me. When we fellowship, we cannot even consider sending them an invitation. We carry the mental, emotional, social and countless other types of weights with us and expect those closest to us to carry them as well. They cannot heal until we are healed. They cannot rejoice until we rejoice. Left, right, left, right, all turn together.

CAN THESE DRY BONES LIVE?

Perhaps this is all resonating with you, and you find yourself saying, 'OK, Aaron! I admit that I have preached a eulogy over _____! I called it dead, preached the funeral, and have invited people to carry it with me. How do I correct this? How do I see life where I have pronounced death? For that, we must return to John, and watch how resurrection power was made available then, and see the far-reaching implications to our disruption sermons!

> [33] When Jesus therefore saw her weeping, and the Jews who came with her also weeping, He was deeply moved in spirit and was troubled, [34] and said, "Where have you laid him?" They said to Him, "Lord, come and see." [35] Jesus wept. [36] So the Jews were saying, "See how He loved him!"

Remember in chapter two, I said that it is what we *do* in the midst of our disruptions that determines the outcome? Jesus's question here gives great indication to that claim. He asks, in essence, '*What did you do* when things got bad?' 'Where have you laid him?' was not a question of location as much as it was a question of expectation. If Lazarus is in the house, you believe what you just said to me. But if he is in a tomb, your proclamations and practices don't quite add up. Nevertheless, what is evident is that God is not insensitive to our suffering. Even when our doubts and fears have resulted in funeral processions, God's love and affection remain.

Being the shortest verse in all of the Bible, John 11:35 is often referenced, but mostly for humorous reasons. People jokingly boast that they have memorized a Bible verse, and then follow up with, 'Jesus wept!' Ironically, they don't know where that passage is found. While this might be the shortest verse, it is packed with power. The reason why Jesus wept would certainly be speculative. Perhaps he wept because he loved Lazarus, as the Jews observantly noted. Knowing that he held the power to resurrect him, I am not sure that this is quite it. I think his weeping may have more to do with disruption and disappointment. He was moved because the ones he loved were suffering, but also a little disappointed that they did not have enough faith in him to keep Lazarus at home. Speculative, but the context definitely renders this theory something worth taking into consideration. The story continues...

> [37] But some of them said, "Could not this man, who opened the eyes of the blind man, have kept this man also from dying?" [38] So Jesus, again being deeply moved within, came to the tomb. Now it was a cave, and a stone was lying against it.

Our questions aren't new. As I stated in chapter two, disruptions can cause us to question God, especially when our conditions don't reflect his character. Whether it be for his seemed inability or apathy, our disruptions are the prosecutors that put God on trial. This crowd is not concerned to see the miracles that Jesus might do; they are more concerned with indicting him on what he could already have done. What they miss is that both are the same Jesus. From this point in the unfolding drama, Jesus takes over. He will revise the sermon and reassign roles.

REWRITE THE SERMON

> ³⁹ Jesus said, "Remove the stone." Martha, the sister of the deceased, said to Him, "Lord, by this time there will be a stench, for he has been dead four days." ⁴⁰ Jesus said to her, "Did I not say to you that if you believe, you will see the glory of God?" ⁴¹ So they removed the stone.

Three powerful words, and he didn't repeat himself. I love this part of the story. Jesus is fully aware of how bad things have gotten. He knew that Lazarus had been dead for some time. Jesus was Jewish, which means that he was privileged to know Jewish customs. The stench of the deceased was not foreign to him. Jesus did not need them to teach him, he needed them to trust him… *'Did I not say…?'* Observe the instruction more closely. Jesus did not instruct them to bring the dead body out. The first command, in fact, has nothing to do with Lazarus. It has everything to do with them. By instructing them to remove the stone, Jesus speaks directly to their obstruction (doubt). He says 'You have to do something about your doubt and fear!'

We too need to learn how to re-write our sermons and preach to our fear. We sing songs about our fear all the time: 'My fear doesn't stand a chance!' 'Fear doesn't live here anymore!' 'Hello fear…apart from you is where I belong!' Great songs! They might even inspire us for a moment. But we need to move beyond the song and get to the sermon! 'Remove the stone!' Very clear command – not simply *move* the stone, as to peek in and see if there is any movement. Do not yell toward the stone, as if to seek a response to your beckoning. You must remove the stone! What a sermon of revival to that thing you have buried! What a message to that which God has created you to do! As long as the stone is in front of the tomb, our doubts and fears are still preaching the sermon. This is only the start of the sermon.

REJOICE IN THE LORD

> ⁴¹ Then Jesus raised His eyes, and said, "Father, I thank You that You have heard Me. ⁴² "I knew that You always hear Me; but because of the people standing around I said it, so that they may believe that You sent Me." ⁴³ When He had said these things, He cried out with a loud voice, "Lazarus, come forth."

Every good sermon has to have *at least* one good praise break! Well, at least that's how it goes in the Pentecostal/Charismatic church. Jesus pauses to praise God in the midst of this sermon, but get this…NO LAZARUS YET! That is difficult! We would have no problem praising and thanking God after Lazarus has come out! This is where the organ starts tuning up and the drummer is rolling doublets on the kick and riding the cymbals. When Lazarus 'comes forth,' the praise team already knows that they had best be on stage, mics in hand, ready to break out in a chorus. But, here, we have a praise break before a miracle. That is true faith: it is the assurance of things hoped for, the conviction of things not seen (Hebrews 11:1). Praise, especially in a disruption, is a sign of faith.

His praise is no superficial mantra of religious jargon. His praise is from a place of history (what God *has* done) and experience (he and God). His praise was not based on what he expected God to do; it was based on what God had already done. The miracle working reputation that preceded him to Bethany, he attributes to the Father. Read through the Gospel of John, and you will find that each time God works a miracle, it is preceded by a command from Jesus. 'Fill the water pots…' and water is turned into wine (John 2). 'Go…' and a noble man's son is healed (John 4). 'Get up…' and a paralytic is healed (John 5). 'Have the people sit down…' and thousands are fed from two fish and five loaves (John 6). The miracles and commands continue throughout John's gospel account. Thus, the personal nature of this praise break. I can only imagine the reason for Jesus's praise; 'Every time I gave a command, in faith, you answered. I praise you because you heard the 'sermons' that I preached to the obstacles, and in turn, you performed the miracle.'

After preaching to the obstruction, and pausing for a praise break, Jesus then preaches to the obvious…the dead. The obstacle is removed, faith is restored, now it's time for these dead bones to come to life: 'Lazarus, come forth!' (Some versions will read, 'come out'). This command is rich with implications. The command is not to merely 'arise' or 'get up'. Literally, Lazarus is commanded to leave the tomb where they have placed him. He is commanded to dissociate himself from the resting place of the dead. He must now join the space of the living. 'Lazarus, you are in the wrong place! Come out here, toward me, where you belong!' What a grand revision to the sermon that Mary and Martha had so boldly preached.

RELEASE THE WEIGHT

> [44] The man who had died came forth, bound hand and foot with wrappings, and his face was wrapped around with a cloth. Jesus said to them, "Unbind him, and let him go." [45] Therefore many of the Jews who came to Mary, and saw what He had done, believed in Him.

Now here is a scene straight out of a movie! It's a hot day in the middle of the afternoon. People are dressed in funeral clothes. Faces are red from tears and wailing for the past few days. Ladies sit in veils, men sit in circles of hushed conversations, remembering their friend. Oh! Here comes the miracle worker...LATE! What!?! Move the stone?! What are you, crazy? It stinks! He's gone! Fine! We'll move it just so that you can pay your last respects, we guess. Suddenly the mourning crowd hears the command, 'Lazarus! Come out here to me!' The conversing men stop. The mourning women lift their veils. Those who removed the stone give another ten yards of space– not knowing what to expect. Without delay, a man comes out. It's not a walk, but a hop, for his feet are bound. He is fully wrapped head to toe. End scene! That's a wrap (unwrap?)!

At this point, Jesus has done his job! Lazarus is no longer dead. He lives. He may need a good bath, as I am sure the cloth still has a stench of death. He may not have full range of mobility, as his hands and feet are bound. Even his vision is obscured as his head is still wrapped. Nevertheless, Lazarus is alive! Hallelujah! We have a problem though. Lazarus is alive but obstacles are preventing him from fully experiencing life. As long as Lazarus is wrapped and bound, the community and the cadence remain, at least to a degree. It is not enough to rewrite the sermon; we must also release the weight.

'Unbind him and let him go.' Two commands from Jesus are necessary for the pallbearers to be released from their commitments. A resurrection without a release is not a life, it is a restriction and a reminder. Until Lazarus is unwrapped, his movements will be restricted. Sure, he can move – he came out of the grave on his own. But we aren't told how long it took; we are only told that he was still bound. Had he worked, he would not be able to return to his job as long as his hands were wrapped. Perhaps he could see partially through the linen, but he certainly would not live as he had before with impaired vision. As a result, he would go through life remembering that he was once dead, but still feeling the effects. As a result of these bandages, he would continue to be a weight – to his sisters and the pallbearers whom they had employed for their dead brother. For the weight to be released, they must remove the obstacles preventing him from fully experiencing life.

WHAT ARE YOU SAYING?

I am sure you are familiar with the proverb that 'death and life are in the power of the tongue' (Proverbs 18:21). This is especially true in disruptions. Too often, our words are words of death. Oftentimes, we are not necessarily trying to be negative or pessimistic; sometimes, we are just trying to be responsible. Our words are meant to mask our emotions and paint the picture that we have everything under control. This artificial sense of peace and responsibility evolves into apathy and abandonment. 'It's OK, I really didn't like that job anyway and I was going to quit.' Or 'I'm glad this business didn't work out, because I don't want to miss the time with family.' How about, 'We should not have gotten married in the first place. We were both too young and immature, so it is good that we are getting divorced.' These are all real statements. Eulogies birthed out of doubt and fear, cloaked in calm control, but revealing apathy and abandonment. Do not let this disruption end in death! What are you saying in this disruption? What are you preaching?

What are the stones that you must preach to? What obstacles have doubt and fear placed in your way? The sermon might begin with 'I need to schedule a meeting!' That meeting might be a meeting of reconciliation, it might be a meeting with an employer or an investor. It might be a meeting with a doctor, or a trainer. Perhaps the rewritten sermon begins with enrollment into a financial stewardship class or becoming part of a small group.

It is not enough to speak to the stones; you should be talking to God! Remember the Psalm that says to bless the Lord, and 'forget not his benefits' (Psalm 103:2)? Perhaps your disruption might demand that you take a pause and get a journal. Maybe a record of God's intervention in your life is long overdue. How many times has God stepped in, even in the slightest way, on your job, in your home, in your ministry? Recall those things and rejoice in God's hand at work in your life!

Don't forget the obvious. Too many people stop at praise, and do not follow through with the words that lead to true resurrection power; 'Lazarus, come forth!' Speak life into that which you have declared dead. Remember that the work God has made you for, he has prepared in advance! Your career is not over, your business endeavors have not come to an end. God is not finished with your marriage. Speak life into those things!

Finally, release the weight! Do not speak life, only to let your job, business, marriage, children, or ministry, remain bound and wrapped in the bandages of fear, suspicion, doubt, comparison, or regret. Unwrap it and let it go! Keep planning, dreaming, moving, working, and believing! Life waits for you on the other side of this thing!

QUESTIONS FOR REFLECTION

1. I argue, in this chapter, that we become preachers when we face disruptions. Think of a current or memorable ***DISRUPTION*** of your own. What are some of the verbal ways in which you 'preached' about your situation? (Reflect back to our big idea, subject, complement for an example). How did your big idea effect the outcome?

2. Illustrated sermons employ people, props, and even places in order to tell a story to communicate a big idea. Oftentimes, we employ the same elements in different ***DISRUPTIONS***. What are some of your go-to elements that help to preach your illustrated ***DISRUPTION*** sermons? (an example might be finances) How are these elements employed? (to further the example, do disruptions often cause you to spend differently? To share differently? etc)

3. It is easy to find inspiration in our society. We see it in social media quotes. We observe it portrayed in sentimental movies and television shows. Certainly, we can hear it on the radio, in our music, and read books on inspiration. Is preaching/declaring life in our disruption necessary, since inspiration is so prevalent? Why do you suppose?

4. Keeping the disruption from question #1 in mind, imagine your sermon being re-written. How might you preach life into that situation, given that you believe that you are God's workmanship, and he has a good purpose for you?

5 DERAILMENT: WHAT ARE YOU THINKING?

> She was driving last Friday on her way to Cincinnati
> on a snow-white Christmas Eve,
> Going home to see her mama and her daddy
> with the baby in the backseat.
> Fifty miles to go, and she was running low on faith and gasoline.
> It'd been a long hard year.
> She had a lot on her mind, and she didn't pay attention;
> she was going way too fast.
> Before she knew it, she was spinning on a thin black sheet of glass.
> She saw both their lives flash before her eyes.
> She didn't even have time to cry.
> She was so scared; she threw her hands up in the air.

These lyrics are the first verse to the song, 'Jesus, Take the Wheel'. If you are like me, you've said the phrase but weren't familiar with the song. Unfortunately, this could also be the soundtrack of our lives when we are facing disruptions; in fact, for many of us it is. On its own, the phrase, 'Jesus, take the wheel!' sounds like a good thing, right? It sounds as if we are surrendering control to God; and, to a degree we are. The problem is not in faithful surrender, it is in failed stewardship.

Thus far, we have discussed two outcomes of a disruption that are not in our favor. Delays are a loss of time, resources, and opportunities. Death is a loss of so much more: dreams, plans, hope, purpose. We now turn our attention to what I suggest may be the most damaging outcome; derailment. Why is it that derailment is so dangerous, more damaging than death or delay? It is because derailments most often produce collateral damage. More than death or delay, derailments lead to innocent casualties. A derailment, by definition, is "the obstruction of a process by diverting it from its intended course."[97] Oftentimes disruptions cause us to divert from our intended course, and in the process, dramatically impact the lives of others.

---

[97] "Derailment," *Apple Dictionary*, 2005-2019.

Consider how this impact might look on a grand, public scale. In 2001, on September 11, flights were diverted from their intended course. Instead of transporting people to their homes, job interviews, family reunions or vacations, these planes were repurposed as weapons of mass destruction. The diversion from the intended course led to thousands of fatalities, and tens of thousands of injuries. That is just the physical damage. Countless are the personal crises that resulted from the catastrophic events that day. Innumerable hours of counseling were needed for survivors and grieving loved ones. What was labeled as the single most deadly terrorist act in America's history was an act of derailment by a relatively small number of individuals.

As I write this chapter, our nation is experiencing derailment of a different type. A Minnesota police officer diverted from his sworn duty to protect and serve all citizens, when he took the life of George Floyd by suffocating him with a knee to the neck. The incident was captured on film and was viewed by millions around the country via social media. Although this incident was not the only act of injustice that the black community had recently faced, still it was an event that became the catalyst for protests and riots in major cities around the country. George Floyd was not the only casualty of officer Chauvin's derailment. While a great number took to the streets in peaceful protests, there were also groups who took arms, in response to police misconduct. Some took to criminal activity and violence. Businesses were vandalized, law enforcement officers attacked, friendships were ruined over opposing views about the subsequent re-emergence of the #BlackLivesMatter movement. Chauvin, and the other officers with him, ultimately would go on to face criminal charges, but still, the collateral damage had been done. The derailment of one individual from his sworn duty impacted him, his colleagues, the individual in his custody, the community, and a ripple effect that this book could not adequately detail.

Derailments are not just public events though. Especially when we are speaking in the context of disruptions, derailments are most often private events with public implications. One spouse's divergence from their covenant in the form of adultery, derails the family. One business owner's divergence from their commitment to ethics and integrity leads to forfeiture of assets, consolidation of business, or bankruptcy. This could leave employees out of work, thus impacting the families of these individuals. A teacher's divergence from a commitment to training and developing, leads to incompetent learning, and a student is unable to enter college.

The scenarios change, but the outcomes are the same. Remember when we unpacked Ephesians 2:10 in chapter one. We are the workmanship of God, created in Christ Jesus, for good works, prepared in advance by God...*so that we would walk in them.* Although we can look at these tragedies and affirm that derailments are problematic, we might too quickly limit derailments to tragic events, and not appreciate the gravity of life lived void of walking in obedience to God. Where we would look at the above-described events as sins of *commission* (the act of doing something wrong), we would do well to consider the sins of *omission* (the act of *not* doing what is *right*) that also lead to derailment!

Some disruptions cause us to blame God and relieve ourselves from any responsibility of stewardship; or worse, we make brash decisions with no thought of the aftermath. The woman in the song quoted above had so much on her mind that it impacted her ability to plan (running low on gas), think (didn't pay attention), and even control herself (going way too fast). Similarly, disruptions can have a dramatic effect on our safety, as well as diminish our sanity. Disruptions can cause us to say, like the chorus of the song, 'I can't do this...I'm letting go.' Letting go sometimes seems like the more spiritually mature thing to do; it is placing our trust in God, and not in ourselves or our efforts. There is a great difference in active trust and anxious thrust. The former is an act of faith, the latter an emotive response to fears and frustrations. In this chapter, we will look at a Biblical account of a disruption that led to derailment, but also witness a realignment in the story! Before we move on, it is important that we see ourselves in the driver's seat, as it relates to navigating the disruptions of our lives; we are the conductors.

CONDUCTORS AND CATASTROPHES

It is difficult to talk about derailment and not think of a train. The very picture that comes to mind, most often, is a train that is riding at excessive speeds, unable to decelerate or perhaps bend the curve of the tracks on which it rides. If you take a moment to read the headlines and interviews surrounding train derailments, the details prove that it is seldom simply a matter of mechanical error. Mechanics are always investigated, but the conductor is as well. In 2013, Fox News reported that a conductor faced multiple negligent homicide charges for a derailment that led to nearly 80 deaths.[98] Excessive speeds prohibited the train from making a turn. The conditions surrounding this derailment sound similar to our above noted song. The conductor found himself in a state where he no longer had control, and thought that the best thing to do was to 'ride it out.' The conditions (speed, mechanics, tracks, weight, and who knows what else) caused the conductor to lose control, and the derailment caused him to lose composure – 79 people dead, 70 people injured, 22 of those in the hospital with critical injuries. It was reported that the conductor stated that he did not want to live after seeing the results.

Some derailments have no passengers, fewer casualties, but the aftermath is still catastrophic. Take, for example, the 2013 derailment in Lac-Megantic, Quebec.[99] Three employees of the railway company faced charges of criminal negligence, after their runaway train carrying crude oil derailed and exploded in a populated city, killing 47 people. Lives were lost and businesses and homes destroyed. Thousands of residents were evacuated. While the men were ultimately acquitted of the charges, BBC News gave accounts of the trial and details surrounding the catastrophe.[100] At 65 miles per hour, the unmanned train served as nothing short of an explosive weapon of mass destruction aimed at the heart of the city. Legally, the men were not guilty of the charges filed against them, but the damaging effects of the derailment are not as easy to dismiss. Families, jobs, and a community were drastically changed.

These are but two stories, amid countless others, where a train derailment ended in innocent casualties, but they help us to understand a profound truth: derailments can lead to casualties whether or not you are carrying passengers. What this means, when we face disruptions, is that it doesn't matter whether we are single or married, managing a team or working independently. The decisions we make, like 'ride it out,' or decisions we neglect to make, like preventing potentially hazardous situations, can lead to catastrophic derailments.

What is most unfortunate is to read through some of the derailment stories and find that at times, the conductor or engineer was not being

---

[98] https://www.foxnews.com/world/spanish-train-conductor-faces-multiple-negligent-homicide-charges-after-accident.
[99] https://www.ctvnews.ca/canada/train-conductor-company-face-charges-in-connection-with-deadly-lac-megantic-derailment-1.1818602.
[100] https://www.bbc.com/news/world-us-canada-42548824.

intentionally neglectful. There are accounts where conductors explain that they thought they had done all the right things. They followed all of the responsible procedures, yet the catastrophe is not avoided. Somehow, doing what seemed right in the moment ends in results that leave a memorable mark on the life of the conductor, a community, and many other lives. Experts looking into the matter from the outside have different opinions on the series of events. It is in the aftermath of the event that alternative scenarios are offered as a means to show how the matter could have been avoided. In the two real-life situations previously noted, experts even refer to the manual or guidelines that would govern such a situation. Scripture is not silent to such matters. As we will soon see, people of the Bible experienced derailments as well.

A KING, A CART, AND A CATASTROPHE

Chapters 4 and 5 of 1 Samuel tell the story of how the ark of the covenant of God was taken from the Israelites. The story has somewhat of a roller coaster effect on the emotions of the reader. Chapter 4 begins with the Israelites setting up camp against the Philistines, but the Philistines overcome them. The Israelites run back to their camp devastated, but the elders have an 'Aha!' moment. They send for the ark. If they have the ark with them, which represents the presence of God, victory would be inevitable, right? Wrong! At first, it seemed as though it worked. The shouts of praise and celebration that went forth at the entry of the ark into the camp scared the Philistines. They recalled that this God of the Israelites was the same one that sent plagues to the Egyptians (vv. 7-8). But they shook off the fear and shook up the Israelites. After beating the Israelites, the Philistines took the ark for themselves.

Chapter 5 reads somewhat like a comedy/sci-fi/cult-type of film. The Philistines take the ark back to Ashdod, and store it in their temple with their god, Dagon. The next morning, the Ashdodites come in to find their god fallen on his face. They fix it, only to come back and find it fallen again the next day, except this time he was missing limbs too. Really, it reminds you of the movie Poltergeist or something. While God was toppling over their idol, his hand was also against the men of the city – resulting in either death or sickness. They had the ark in their possession for seven months. Finally, they have had enough! They realize that God would not share a space with their false god, so they send the ark back to the Israelites, to the Ekronites.

In chapters 6 and 7, the ark makes its way back to Israel, finally settling for twenty years at the home of Abinadab with a man named Eleazar. At that time, Israel had no king; they were a theocratic nation: under the rulership of God and leadership of Judges. As the ark finally comes back to Israel, Samuel the prophet is judge over Israel. As the story progresses, this whole issue of the ark is seemingly forgotten. Samuel has two sons that he appoints as judges, and they turn out to be shady characters. Soon Israel demands a king just like the other nations. Saul is chosen to be king. The rest of the book of 1 Samuel is about battles, victories, failures, God's selection of a new King (David), and the seemingly unending rage that Saul has against him. David won't rule *all* of Israel until the 5th chapter of 2 Samuel. His first major act of reform, as king, was to bring the ark back. The abbreviated record of events is found in 2 Samuel 6, but to help us in a case study of the derailment that takes place, we must turn to 1 Chronicles. There, we are privy to the dialogue that leads up to bringing the ark home to Jerusalem, where it belongs.

> **1 Chronicles 13:1–14 (NASB)**
>
> [1] Then David consulted with the captains of the thousands and the hundreds, even with every leader. [2] David said to all the assembly of Israel, "If it seems good to you, and if it is from the LORD our God, let us send everywhere to our kinsmen who remain in all the land of Israel, also to the priests and Levites who are with them in their cities with pasture lands, that they may meet with us; [3] and let us bring back the ark of our God to us, for we did not seek it in the days of Saul." [4] Then all the assembly said that they would do so, for the thing was right in the eyes of all the people. [5] So David assembled all Israel together, from the Shihor of Egypt even to the entrance of Hamath, to bring the ark of God from Kiriath-jearim.

It would seem that David had all his bases covered. As king, he recognizes that the previous administration was neglectful in a very important matter. Surely you didn't think that political drama started with democrats and republicans! No, David was not throwing away his shot! Now it was his turn to lead, and he was going to do it better than his predecessor. David had to make sure. Is this the right move? Were his motives pure? So says the text that David took it to counsel, and he took it to prayer. And

EVERYONE was in agreement about it. Going into this with all his t's crossed and i's dotted, what could go wrong? I'm sure it's no spoiler alert that something's going to go wrong...terribly wrong! This is the reason for choosing this story. When you look at the front matter – the meetings, consultations, collaboration, and history, how could this story go south?

That's exactly how it is for us sometimes! Disruptions can come when all of our motives are right, we've done our homework, listened to mentors, and even sought the mind of God on a matter. Again, consider David's pursuit... We are bringing the presence of God home... *WHAT CAN GO WRONG?!* It is, however, an uncomfortable reality that disruptions come, *even when* we are trying to draw closer to God. Some might even argue that they come *especially when* we are. Maybe you've experienced that before; your finances were great until you decided that you were going to honor God with your wealth. You had no problem living an exciting life as a single person, but the moment that you decided that you wanted to live a life *fully* committed to God, the disruptions came; all your single friends were getting married, all of your favorite shows seem to lean heavier toward romance, and God forbid you show up to another family or church event without a plus one! David is at the threshold, so it seems, of such a situation.

> ⁶ David and all Israel went up to Baalah, *that is,* to Kiriath-jearim, which belongs to Judah, to bring up from there the ark of God, the LORD who is enthroned *above* the cherubim, where His name is called. ⁷ They carried the ark of God on a new cart from the house of Abinadab, and Uzza and Ahio drove the cart. ⁸ David and all Israel were celebrating before God with all *their* might, even with songs and with lyres, harps, tambourines, cymbals and with trumpets. ⁹ When they came to the threshing floor of Chidon, Uzza put out his hand to hold the ark, because the oxen nearly upset *it.* ¹⁰ The anger of the LORD burned against Uzza, so He struck him down because he put out his hand to the ark; and he died there before God.

Everything in me wants to pause at this point and touch on some parenting lessons here. Uzza could have been a kid when the ark came to his home. Maybe he had grown too familiar with the ark and the route on which they walked. If only his parents had raised him to understand holy things... But I digress – there is a rich enough lesson here.

What is incredible here is the fact that there is a worship service going on that would give Azusa, Megafest, and Kanye West all a run for their money! The king and the whole nation are celebrating! It's a worship service parade! And yet, something happens that upsets God! As I read this part of the story, I am reminded of the popular worship song that says, 'This is how I fight my battles!' I can't help but point out a truth that this story conveys, and that is the fact that praise will not stop, nor will it prevent every disruption. Don't get me wrong, Scripture is replete with instances of disruption breaking worship! While such cases do exist, we must recognize that there are cases when God is not moved by our song, but by our seeking him. In fact, there is another important lesson that we may observe: their very excitement gave them a sense of familiarity with the things of God that became unhealthy, and they neglected to give the ark the respect God demanded. We will soon see that this was not the case of God throwing a divine temper tantrum, but a case of careless procedure.

If you are reading this story the way that I have so many times, you have probably pointed out the disruption – the falling of the ark. The Ark, however is not the disruption of this story, it is only a catalyst. The real disruption is God's response to Uzzah's attempted recovery. Uh-oh! Lesson alert…but you're used to this by now! Disruptions can come when we are trying to draw closer to God. Praise and worship are not guaranteed defenses against disruptions. Sometimes disruptions are the very hand of God himself stepping into our situations, plans, and agendas in order to get our attention. Here again we have to be careful that we are not reading that truth into every single disruption we face. God will cause some, others he will allow, but as we have already established, he is still God in any event. So, the disruption in this event is the very hand of God inflicting death; and, this is not the first time. Read 1 Samuel 4-7 and watch how many people died in relation to this ark! One thing is historically clear: God takes his presence very seriously, and he takes lives, or at least inflicts some degree of discomfort in the lives of those who do not. His 'outburst' of anger is perhaps best understood taking history into account.

> [11] Then David became angry because of the LORD's outburst against Uzza; and he called that place Perez-uzza to this day. [12] David was afraid of God that day, saying, "How can I bring the ark of God home to me?" [13] So David did not take the ark with him to the city of David, but took it aside to the house of Obed-edom the Gittite. [14] Thus the

> ark of God remained with the family of Obed-edom in his house three months; and the LORD blessed the family of Obed-edom with all that he had.

Some Bible translations make a note in the margins, that Perez-uzza means 'breakthrough of Uzzah' or 'God broke through Uzzah.' Here we see David going through emotions typical in a disruption, and while 'in his feelings,' names the place Perez-uzza.

WHEN GOD BREAKS THROUGH

When God allows a disruption, or creates one, what goes through your mind? For David, he threw his hands up like the song at the opening of this chapter, and simply says, *'I CAN'T!'* He puts it all on God. In his anger and fear, he abandons ship, as if he is the only one that came out to get the ark. He makes a decision, as if he is the only one impacted by his decision. Can you imagine being the family that came out of the house, walked about a 12-mile journey… singing, praising, supporting the king at this moment? Imagine walking with your children, explaining to them the significance of this moment. You're telling them the stories of how the Philistines took it, but God rattled their gods, and then the journey of it coming back home.

No way will you leave out the story of the 50,000+ kinfolk that you lost when they *looked* into the ark. And now, someone reaches out to *touch* it, and God kills him. You've been waiting 20 years for the ark to return. It's not that you are insensitive to what just happened. Let's take a little time, figure out what we are going to do – but let's get this thing home, right? Then the king shuts down the party, sends the band home, and says, 'Just leave the blasted thing over there with Obed!' DERAILMENT!!! But the derailment doesn't stop there! There is a detail implied here in 1 Chronicles that is stated *explicitly* in 2 Samuel.

> **2 Samuel 6:12 (NASB)**
> [12] Now it was told King David, saying, "The LORD has blessed the house of Obed-edom and all that belongs to him, on account of the ark of God." David went and brought up the ark of God from the house of Obed-edom into the city of David with gladness.

For THREE MONTHS, the city is derailed from the presence of God because David made a hasty decision in the midst of a disruption. Look what has happened in 90 days!!!! OBED now enjoys what should have come to the house of David, to the city of Jerusalem. Make no mistake, it is because of the ark being in his home that Obed-edom is blessed – and it is no secret matter! It was public enough that word got back to King David. Imagine again being one of those who had traversed afar with singing and praise to get the ark and witness the king take his hands off the wheel. Now you are hearing stories of blessings coming from Obed's house. Tough!

Let's pause for a moment and come out of the Old Testament into the 21st Century, because it is so easy to read too swiftly pass this information without appreciating this span of time. Remember the catalyst for this book is the Covid-19 pandemic that has swept the globe. At the writing of this chapter, we are just hitting the 90-day window of the pandemic. It is unfathomable, all of the changes in our nation and abroad, that have happened since the start of this thing. 90 days is a significant span of time, whether you are counting days of blessing, or days of a pandemic. David and the people in the city of Jerusalem missed the blessings that came with the presence of God, because David let go of the wheel.

If Obed-edom's recent blessings evidenced anything, it's the fact that disruptions don't always mean stop! Sometimes they mean REALIGN! What David sought to do was actually a good thing – something that God would indeed bless. God caused this disruption early in David's career as king, and there was great reason for it. The previous king was a bit lax when it came to the commands of God, and it cost him his throne. David, God's chosen king, began his reign restoring Godly order, but he was not careful in the way he went about it; the result was a disruption that led to derailment of the blessings of God for him, and for the people.

Most of us have caused derailments in our lifetimes. I have made a couple of hasty investment decisions in response to financial disruptions, causing derailments of future opportunities and security for my family. I have faced emotional disruptions, and in my unbridled efforts to change my circumstances, ran myself off course, causing a derailment that adversely impacted my family, my ministry, and the lives of others whom God had placed in my care. Think of the 'derailments' that you have been a victim of, or that you have caused. Divorce is a derailment. Addictions cause derailments. Bankruptcy, sometimes, is a derailment. Incarceration is certainly a derailment. When we really consider all we have experienced in our life, very few of us can honestly say that we have not felt the impact of a derailment.

The beautiful reality is that our derailments are almost never permanent. When we read the stories of derailments in the news, the impact is arguably irreversible, particularly in the case of casualties. When we consider our 'disruption' derailments in life, we have an opportunity to pull the train back on track. Can you imagine how the headlines would change if the conductors were able to put a derailed train back on the tracks and reverse the damages that it caused? What if I told you that we could change *our* headlines!? All it takes is a little realignment.

REALIGNMENT: GETTING BACK ON TRACK

Our thoughts are important to God. This claim is evidenced by the many passages that speak to how we think (Psalm 139:23-24; Romans 12:2; 1 Corinthians 1:10) and what we think (Joshua 1:8; Mark 7:20-23; Philippians 4:8). When we find ourselves in a disruption, it is our thinking that really takes a hit. We begin to assess things like our situation, our value, and our purpose. We ultimately assess the ways and the wisdom of God. Our thoughts toward God have the most potential of derailment, and therefore it is by rightly thinking of God that will bring us back on track. As this story of the ark of the covenant of God progresses, we will witness how king David realigns himself, thus changing the headlines. It all starts with how he thinks about God, and the things of God. May this be our resolve when we know that our decisions have caused or are on the verge of causing a derailment – regardless of the size. Let us return to Scripture and learn how we can realign our lives, as David did.

CONSIDER: Think carefully about God & his Word

The very first thing that we must do is *consider*. This should not come as a surprise to us; we are instructed in James chapter 1 to *'Consider it pure joy...'* when we face trials, or disruptions. We must not misunderstand what it is that we are considering though; James is not just instructing us to try and play mind games with our circumstances and live in denial of what is happening to or around us. Rather, he is saying that we must give serious thought to what God's intended outcome is for the matter. Better stated, we must fix our mind rightly on God, his love, his character, and his Word; that is, who he is, what he does, what he has purposed, and what he demands.

How or what does this disruption cause you to think of God? How does it affect what you believe about him, or his Word? How does this disruption interpret Ephesians 2:10? Can you look at this situation and still affirm that you are the workmanship of God, made in Christ for good works? This is what God's Word says, this is how he assesses you even in the midst of your disruption. OR are you allowing Ephesians 2:10 to interpret this disruption? Truth be told, we often allow the circumstances of our life to interpret Scripture, when it is God's Word that ought to give order and clarity to the circumstances of our life. What is needed as a discipline, educators in practical ministry call 'theological reflection.' Theological reflection is when we step back from a situation (especially a disruption), acknowledge our thoughts, beliefs, and emotions, and bring those into submissive dialogue with the "standard of God's truth as revealed in God's Word."[101] Watch what happens when David gives himself over to theological reflection.

> **1 Chronicles 15:1–3 (NASB)**
> [1] Now David built houses for himself in the city of David; and he prepared a place for the ark of God and pitched a tent for it. [2] Then David said, "No one is to carry the ark of God but the Levites; for the LORD chose them to carry the ark of God and to minister to Him forever." [3] And David assembled all Israel at Jerusalem to bring up the ark of the LORD to its place which he had prepared for it.

Granted, his reflection was not immediate – the ark remained for three months. But in that time, David did some deep searching, (remember, he was angry and afraid), and changed his actions. Now, David is not lost in his feelings! Before, he was angry with God and afraid of God, but now he is once again focused on his mission. This time, the mission will be a little different. Now he has considered the holiness of God, and that if he had only slowed down and treated the ark as a holy thing in the first place, the outcome of the last attempt would have been better. Notice what David was doing since this disruption. It is evident that he considered the holiness of

---

[101] Jim L. Wilson and Earl Waggoner, *A Guide to Theological Reflection: A Fresh Approach for Practical Ministry Courses and Theological Field Education* (Grand Rapids, MI: Zondervan Academic, 2020), 28-33.

God, and what that holiness demanded. His consideration was evidenced by his preparation and evaluation.

He first realized that although bringing the ark home was a great idea, and something that would be pleasing to God, the task was not to be taken lightly. He recognized a lack of stewardship in this noble quest; he hadn't adequately prepared a place, nor the people. Now in 1 Chronicles 15, he not only prepared a place for it, but he reminded the people how it ought to be transported. Only certain individuals were to carry the ark. Whether on a euphoric high or dismal low, we must remember that "emotions are strong drivers of [actions] and can hijack the best intentions or prompt risky actions."[102] For David, the high of bringing back the ark hijacked his actions, and the low of God's killing Uzzah did the same. This emotional hijacking is quite normal, especially when we face disruptions.

CONFORM: Total alignment with holiness

Consideration should lead us to conformity. #NailedIt is one of Karen's favorite shows on Netflix. The popular streaming show is named after the trending hashtag in social media, where home bakers try and replicate a culinary masterpiece that they saw online or in a store. Karen is a queen of cakes. She is known to get random text messages or messages through social media, with a photo of a dessert, asking if she can replicate it for a birthday, anniversary, or event. She is so good at it that she can replicate these dishes just by looking at the photos. That is not the concept of the #NailedIt social media trend, nor the streaming show on Netflix. Both focus on the horrendous, epic #FailedIt attempts to replicate the inspiring dish.

Three contestants compete for a $10,000 prize, among other less expensive but noteworthy prizes for the baker's kitchen. The contestants are just average home bakers; they are not pastry chefs, caterers, or bakery workers. They might be stay-at-home moms, teachers, single dads, engineers – you name it. Given the general and diverse nature of the contestants, it would seem that they would do their best to win the cash prize. Ironically, each contestant has every item that the dish they are trying to replicate calls for. More than having every item, each workstation is equipped with a digital tablet having step by step directions on how to create the dish. It is uncanny

---

[102] Wilson and Waggoner, *Theological Reflection*, 47.

how many contestants read a line on the directions, and blatantly ignore it with statements like:

> "ONE cup of sugar!?! Oh no!!! I LOVE my sugar... I'm using TWO!"

> "Roll the fondant? Well, I don't have time for that – I will just use edible spray paint."

> "Let cool... You know what, I don't let my cakes cool at home... and folks love it!"

Seriously, I cannot make this up! TEN THOUSAND DOLLARS on the line, and you want to go off-script with how you feel, what time you think you have, and what other people say!? What is most interesting is that the dishes they are trying to make were prepared by one of the judges. See the irony here – a judge has invited you to participate in a competition where all you need do is follow the instructions that he prepared before you showed up as a contestant. A disruption comes by error, lack of time or knowledge, or going off-script, lessening the chance at securing the prize. Sound familiar?

It never fails; one of the judges will comment on a technique that was missed, a step that was ignored, or a substitute that was wrongly used. The one who goes home with the prize is the one who stayed closer to the directions – and even that looks like a train wreck. When we consider the ways of God and the Word of God, the only right response is to conform to his ways. We must remember that he is the preparer of our ways, and thus even in a disruption we must follow his directions for holiness. This is exactly what David did when he went back and processed what had taken place, and what he must do. In his theological reflection, he recalled that God had a prescribed order of how the ark was to be treated and transported, and that prescription had not been followed. Look at the instructions that God gave to Moses when the ark was first constructed, and then see how David specifically instructed the Levites.

> **Exodus 25:10–15 (NASB)**
>
> [10] "They shall construct an ark of acacia wood two and a half cubits long, and one and a half cubits wide, and one and a half cubits high. [11] "You shall overlay it with pure gold, inside and out you shall overlay it, and you shall

> make a gold molding around it. [12] "You shall cast four gold rings for it and fasten them on its four feet, and two rings shall be on one side of it and two rings on the other side of it. [13] "You shall make poles of acacia wood and overlay them with gold. [14] "You shall put the poles into the rings on the sides of the ark, to carry the ark with them. [15] "The poles shall remain in the rings of the ark; they shall not be removed from it.

The key to this passage is found in verses 13-15. Remember, when David first went to get the ark, it was placed on a new cart, driven by oxen. The instructions given by God were that there would be permanent poles protruding from the ark. After further investigation, we will see why.

> **Numbers 7:7–9 (NASB)**
>
> [7] Two carts and four oxen he gave to the sons of Gershon, according to their service, [8] and four carts and eight oxen he gave to the sons of Merari, according to their service, under the direction of Ithamar the son of Aaron the priest. [9] But he did not give any to the sons of Kohath because theirs was the service of the holy objects, which they carried on the shoulder.

The poles extending from the ark were not for decoration! They served a distinct purpose. It was by these poles that the Levites would carry the ark when it was in transit. Or at least that is what God had purposed, but again – our emotions can sometimes hijack our actions. Caught up in the emotional high of bringing the ark back home after two decades, David and the people went off-script in transporting the ark – #NAILEDIT! As we continue the story, as recorded in 1 Chronicles 15, we see that David realigns himself. No more being controlled by feelings and emotions; he is going to do things by the book.

> **1 Chronicles 15:11–14 (NASB)**
>
> [11] Then David called for Zadok and Abiathar the priests, and for the Levites, for Uriel, Asaiah, Joel, Shemaiah, Eliel and Amminadab, [12] and said to them, "You are the heads of the fathers' households of the Levites; consecrate

> yourselves both you and your relatives, that you may bring up the ark of the LORD God of Israel to the place that I have prepared for it. [13] "Because you did not carry it at the first, the LORD our God made an outburst on us, for we did not seek Him according to the ordinance." [14] So the priests and the Levites consecrated themselves to bring up the ark of the LORD God of Israel.

Notice how David moves from information (What has God commanded, concerning this?) to transformation (What must we do, considering what God has commanded?). Both are essential to realignment. Remember the old saying, 'If at first you don't succeed, try…try again!'? That's great wisdom for a four-year-old learning to tie their shoes or a six-year-old trying to ride a bike without training wheels. When we are going through a disruption, trying and trying again is not always the answer – in fact, it is seldom the answer! We must step back and consider how God may be trying to get our attention. Have we ignored the holy things? No, not every disruption is God 'breaking through' in response to our neglect, but rest assured, every disruption is worthy of an intentional theological reflection. Only then can we rightly conclude that our actions, our beliefs, and our convictions are co-aligned. Still, there is one final stage to our realignment.

CARRY ON: You have a destination to reach!

> **1 Chronicles 15:15–16, 25-26 (NASB)**
>
> [15] The sons of the Levites carried the ark of God on their shoulders with the poles thereon, as Moses had commanded according to the word of the LORD. [16] Then David spoke to the chiefs of the Levites to appoint their relatives the singers, with instruments of music, harps, lyres, loud-sounding cymbals, to raise sounds of joy.
>
> [25] So *it was* David, with the elders of Israel and the captains over thousands, who went to bring up the ark of the covenant of the LORD from the house of Obed-edom with joy. [26] Because God was helping the Levites who were carrying the ark of the covenant of the LORD, they sacrificed seven bulls and seven rams.

There is no crafty way to say it...David goes and gets the ark! In his fear and anger (1 Chronicles 13), David asks 'How *can* I?!' But now, in chapter 15, after considering the ways of God and the Word of God concerning that which he had endeavored to do, David's question changes to 'How *should* I?!' Caught up in his feelings, David misreads the death of Uzzah; if *this* happened, then maybe I was wrong to even attempt this. Remember, we spoke earlier about false-reads in a situation. It is only by a process of theological reflection whereby David was able to recall, reassess, and reposition so he can resume what he had originally set out to do.

Isn't it interesting how everything seems to fall in line when David gets his thinking right? When he considers what God's command is, the venture is successful. Not only did they bring the ark back in the right fashion, but they were still worshipping. There wasn't a fear of the ark tumbling, or a trepidation that God might 'break through' again, because David knew what went wrong before and he conformed to what he knew they were to do. His thoughts, rightly fixed, informed his actions, rightly executed. What was a derailment before, resulting in a lack of blessing for the citizens of Jerusalem, was now a successful operation. It was so successful in fact, that Scripture records – God even helped them carry it. This is what happens when we *consider* and *conform* to the ways of God – he gives us the means to carry on, and then he walks *with* us!

WHAT ARE YOU THINKING?

If you go back and look at the articles on the derailments mentioned earlier, you will encounter a similarity, and I am sure you would find it in other stories. The conductor thought _____. Perhaps they thought they had things under control. Perhaps they thought that things would work themselves out. Perhaps they thought that there was nothing that they could do. Whatever they were thinking, their conclusions informed their actions or inactions. The resultant derailment gives evidence that what they were thinking was inaccurate. Something about the procedure was wrong, or perhaps an assessment of the equipment was misinformed. The same can be said about our decision making when we face disruptions.

Whether God has allowed the disruption (the Oxen trips), or he causes it (Uzzah is dead), we must not forget that God is present in our disruptions. Through considering his Word, we can gain a better perspective of the situation. We must remember that derailments start in the mind: they begin the moment that we think of God through the lens of our disruptions instead of processing our disruptions through the lens of God's Word. Our thoughts inform our actions, and when those thoughts violate the Word and will of God, there will always be collateral damage. Think of all the decisions that you have made in the past, that you *thought* would hurt no one, only to find out how many people were actually affected by your decision. You may be inclined to believe that your singleness, or your seemingly insignificant position at work, or in the ministry lessen the collateral damage, but to suppose that would be a grave error.

Every derailed train started in a static, non-moving position. Derailments are not calculated, unless planned by a terrorist or an extremist. They are catastrophes in motion. The same is true for our derailing decisions that we make in a disruption. Such actions are not made by a well-rested, thoughtful individual who has paused to reflect and seek the mind of God in a matter. In fact, one of the greatest reasons that we often end up in derailments when we face a disruption is that we are not rested. Consider once again the lyrics to 'Jesus, Take the Wheel!' While the song is a fictitious scenario, the reality of the song is anything but. Curtis Zackery explains his experience in this regard: "I often encounter people from all walks of life who identify themselves as followers of Jesus who say that they don't know if they can "do it" anymore.[103] While the 'it' he refers to is the Christian life, everyone goes through 'it,' Christians and non-Christians alike! Upon further investigation, he finds that the reason for this feeling of abandoning all things is due to a lack of rest. Imagine how many derailments we might avoid if we simply learned to slow down and rest! Imagine if we took time to stop and think. Perhaps that is why God gave us a command to observe a day of rest – treat it as holy. From the story of the Ark, we see what happens when we think differently about things that God has declared holy.

---

[103] Zackery, *Soul Rest*, 2.

QUESTIONS FOR REFLECTION

1. *'Jesus, take the wheel!'* sounds much like a cry of faithful surrender, but it is not. How do you differentiate between faithful surrender and simply giving up?

2. Derailments are decisions made by one person that have adverse effects on innocent others. Can you think of some subtle derailments that you have experienced in your life where you were one of the 'innocent others'? What do you suppose was the disruption that caused this derailment?

3. What are some of the initial thoughts that go through your mind when first encountering a disruption?

4. Having resolved that disruptions are at least allowed by God, if not created by him, do any of the thoughts that you listed need editing? What passages of Scripture might help you to edit them best?

5. In the disruption(s) you have been thinking about and listing as you read through the previous chapters, which do you find most challenging:

    a. Considering the character, care, and concern that God has for you, even in the midst of your disruption?

    b. Conforming to his standard of holiness, and whatever process that he chooses to move you further along in your purpose? Why is this so challenging?

6. Every derailed train started in a static, non-moving position. Think about the non-moveable elements (or non-moving states of moveable elements/figures) in the disruption(s) you have faced. Are there any preventative measures that you might think of that may help to potentially avoid similar disruptions in the future?

6 DESTINY: WHAT ARE YOU AIMING FOR?

As we turn our attention to the final disruption outcome that I propose, let's take a moment to review the outcomes that we have discussed thus far. First, our disruptions can end in delay; that means when it is all said and done, what we went through was nothing more than a complete waste of time. If you recall, I presented the case that it is the object of our waiting that determines whether our disruptions will end in delay – so, what are you waiting for? Second, we learned that disruptions can sometimes end in death; perhaps not a physical death, but death of a relationship, of a career, of a vision or dream. Remember, it is the words we say (preachers) and the weight that we carry (pallbearers) that determines whether our disruptions end in death – so, what are you saying? In the last chapter, we looked at the most dangerous outcome, derailment. This outcome is the most dangerous because it adversely impacts innocent people: our spouse, children, employees, co-workers, church, etc. What was it that determined this particular outcome? It is our thoughts – how we assess what we are going through, how we view God's hand in the matter – so, what are you thinking?

But enough of all the warning signs, you're probably thinking. At this point, we get it – disruptions can possibly end badly, but surely if God causes all things to work together for the good of those who love him and are called for his purpose (Romans 8:28), and he has prepared what our good works are in advance (Ephesians 2:10), how can we see the purpose and plan of God fulfilled in our disruptions? How can we navigate through them in such a way that God is glorified, and we are assured that we have navigated this situation as he would have us? This chapter looks at the outcome that we all desire – destiny.

GOING FOR GOALS, NOT GOLD!

I am not an athlete. To be honest, I really do not enjoy watching sports. I'd rather relax in my 'book nook' with some jazz and call it a day! I do, however, enjoy watching the Olympics. Summer or winter does not matter – as long as the nations converge to compete! Being the grandson of a Jamaican immigrant, I always cheer for two teams – USA and Jamaica! One of my favorite movies, in fact, is Cool Runnings – where a group of Jamaican boxcar derby racers start a bobsled team. If there were ever a sport that I think I would like to try, it would be bobsledding. It looks simple enough – you rock the sled, give a nice running start, then it is just a matter of gravity and bending with the turns, right? I am sure any experienced bobsledder would cringe at such a limited view of the sport. There is one sport, however, that never EVER interests me – running! Sprints, marathons, dashes, it doesn't matter; I hate running! To be honest, I think that I hate running because I am not really that fast. I am fairly strong, but my strength does nothing for me when it comes to running against someone who is just fast! It is interesting that Paul would use racing as a picture to describe our life-experience, particularly a life lived unto God.

> **1 Corinthians 9:23–27 (NASB)**
>
> [23] I do all things for the sake of the gospel, so that I may become a fellow partaker of it. [24] Do you not know that those who run in a race all run, but only one receives the prize? Run in such a way that you may win. [25] Everyone who competes in the games exercises self-control in all things. They then do it to receive a perishable wreath, but we an imperishable. [26] Therefore I run in such a way, as not without aim; I box in such a way, as not beating the air; [27] but I discipline my body and make it my slave, so that, after I have preached to others, I myself will not be disqualified.

Paul has gone full-on Olympiad in his description of life: running, competing, boxing, discipline. Paul is not without company. The writer of Hebrews exhorts the reader to 'run, with endurance, the race set before us' (Hebrews 12:1). So, maybe running is not all that bad. Paul, as well as the author of Hebrews, saw something that was noteworthy about the Olympic games – it was about much more than the observed sport. To be clear, the Olympic games of ancient Greece are nothing like what we watch on our big 4K HDTV's today! I am not even convinced that our most colorfully imaginative depictions of the ancient games do justice. There are some similarities between modern and ancient games; for example, see the description of the ancient Olympic athlete, and you might notice the similarity.

> [A]s the individuals, who obtained the prizes in these games, received great honours and rewards, not only from their fellow-citizens, but also from foreign states, those

persons who intended to contend for the prizes made extraordinary efforts to prepare themselves for the contest; and it was soon found that, unless they subjected themselves to a severer course of training than was afforded by the ordinary exercises of the gymnasia, they would not have any chance of gaining the victory. Thus arose a class of individuals, to whom the term *athletae* was appropriated, and who became, in course of time, the only persons who contended in the public games.[104]

All the sacrifice and training that goes into the Olympic games is not about the gold medal – it is about what the gold medal brings. In fact, it might come as a surprise that the 2016 Summer Olympic gold medal was valued at less than $600.[105] *Wait a minute, you mean that people work hard, train hard, endure bruises, sprains, and blisters for years on end to win a measly medal that is not even worth a grand?!* Oh, that is just a piece of the sacrifice! Some even choose meaningless part-time jobs for several years on end, earning just enough to make ends meet so that they can train! CNBC reported that some athletes might raise money through crowd-funding platforms.[106]

All of these sacrifices are necessary if they want to receive the gold – and believe me, they do! As much as I don't like running, a younger me might be inclined to take interest in the sport, since Olympic gold medalist Usain Bolt secured $30 Million in endorsements after the 2016 Summer Olympics in Rio (Go Jamaica!). Of course, these athletes are not simply trying to make extra cash. Being a gold medalist means international notoriety, respect, and honor – not just for the individual, but also the nation for which they are competing. For some it might be even deeper; they might be running, swimming, serving, or bobsledding for both their nation and their race.

---

[104] William Smith, "ATHLE′TAE," ed. William Smith, *Dictionary of Greek and Roman Antiquities* (Boston: Little, Brown, and Company, 1865), 167.
[105] This value was reported by *Forbes*. https://www.forbes.com/sites/anthonydemarco/2016/08/05/what-is-the-true-value-of-the-rio-olympics-goldmedal/#4308f2ba79d2.
[106] https://www.cnbc.com/2018/02/16/how-much-olympic-athletes-get-paid.html.

What has any of this information to do with disruptions and destiny? Everything! The writer of Hebrews really brings this to light by expounding on how we ought to engage in this life that we live, even during disruptions. Hebrews 12:1-2 tells us that not only are we to run with endurance, but Jesus is offered as a prototypical athlete, after whom we are to pattern ourselves. Though it was the expected plan of God for our redemption, we can still rightly view the cross as Jesus' disruption. It was a journey marked with pain and suffering – one that had the potential to defy the leadership (...*if you are willing, remove this cup from me...* Luke 22:42), yet with a fixed gaze on what was ahead, he endured the cross (...*yet, not my will but yours be done*). His goal was not an emblem, but eternity. The cross on which he hung was of no significant value – it was old, rugged wood. The salvific work which was done on that cross was absolutely priceless! The nails that pierced him could be smelted and repurposed – but his sacrifice will never be reproduced.

Our model, then, is not Usain Bolt, Kevin Durant, the Williams sisters, Michael Phelps, or even the Jamaican bobsled team. Our model is Christ – the ultimate Olympian! No sacrifice that we would ever make compares to dying an innocent death on a cross for the sins of the world! No medal that we could ever win will compare to the redemption of a world! But therein lies the beauty of living out our purpose as established by God through Jesus! Paul says it best in Philippians 3:10-12: he wants to know Jesus 'in the fellowship of his sufferings,' and subsequently 'attain to the resurrection of the dead.' For this, Paul says 'I press on...that I might lay hold.' What that means in a nutshell is that Paul is committed to running, knowing that there will be disruptions along the way, pressing toward what will be his ultimate prize – participation in that for which Jesus ran his race! Although our disruptions differ, we all share in the same prize. The ultimate prize at the end of our 'race' is eternity with the one who ran before us! So let us press toward *our* destiny! *How is that done, exactly?* Just as Paul instructed young Timothy, 'if anyone competes as an athlete, he does not win the prize unless he competes according to the rules' (2 Timothy 2:5). We need to look at Scripture to determine exactly what those rules are.

RULES AND REGULATIONS

At the Power Company Kids Club, we probably have no less than 328 different ways in which you can run a race. We have bubblegum races, egg races, cart races, scooter races, sack races (sounds like Forest Gump... shrimp-kabobs, shrimp creole, shrimp gumbo...). You get the point – we have tons of races! It doesn't matter what kind of race; we start every single game the same way. Everyone has to put one finger in the air, and whoever is on mic will say, '*On your MARK... Getttttt SET...*' No one ever knows how long this next part takes, but they tell the kids, '*When my hand drops... GO!*' We will not start a game any other way! In fact, when I first started working at PCKC, I counted down a game, (*3, 2, 1...*) and was immediately scolded by a crowd of children! Who knew such an old-fashioned practice would be so critical to the program?

We've become so used to these words as kids, that the weight of them is lost as adults. When I am playing with my daughters, I will admit to even being a little lazy with it; speaking in shorthand, '*Mark, Set, Go!*' And they are none the wiser; as far as they are concerned, we are just running around in the grass, or scooting their little toys across the floor. When we look at our journey through life, as a race, this 'call to action' carries a bit of weight! We cannot embrace them '*short-handedly*', for to do so would sacrifice an important part of our adherence to the regulations of the race, if you will. When we say 'On your mark...' we are summoning all participants to get to the place where they need to be, in order to begin the race. 'Get set...' is more than a heads up that 'go' is on the horizon! Getting set means digging your heels in, tightening your grip, getting just a little lower, or raising your head just a bit higher. It is that last bit of preparation before you embark on your fast-paced journey! Finally, '*Go!!!*' The command that every other command has prepared us for...execution!

When we talk about rules and regulations in this race of life, we can sometimes complicate things! I believe that just mastering *On your mark... Get set... Go!* will place many of us in position for success! If we are to truly make our disruptions defining moments that lead us to our destiny, we must master the disciplines of getting in place, getting in position, and going for the prize! If we are going to see our disruption end in destiny, then we must repurpose the situation; we must view it not as a disruption, but as a *defining moment*. Remember, we've defined disruption as any hardship (event, action, word, or thought) which has the effect of temporarily or permanently distorting the workmanship (person), disconnecting the relationship (created in Christ), dismantling the craftsmanship (to do *good* works), denying the authorship (*God* prepared beforehand), and defying leadership (that we *should* walk in them) that our life ought to reflect. A defining moment is an event which informs or determines all subsequently related occurrences.

We have all experienced defining moments in our lives. High marks in school might have a dramatic impact on how we learn. Yet for some, it was being told that they would never amount to anything that pushed them harder, fueling their academic success. Perhaps it was the first time you scored a winning point for your team, and from that point on you knew you wanted to be a professional athlete. Certain reactions from our spouse can inform future romantic advances (or avoidances). I remember Karen once telling me how much she liked when I wore suits... I guess I heard her *too* loud and clear... I was wearing a suit for everything! Walmart? Suit! Doctors' office? Suit! Mowing the lawn? Sweats and a t-shirt, but after I showered...SUIT! OK, maybe that was a stretch, but you get the point. We all have defining moments.

Not all defining moments lead to joy, romance, and success. Some defining moments are interpreted as disruptions, and thus end in tragedy, to some degree. Financial hardship can be a defining moment. Failure is certainly one. Marital or relational crises, health concerns, job loss, and others. Some have had their lives wrecked over one or more of these defining moments, because they did not see them as defining moments. These events seem more like disruptions! In all reality, they are; however, I would argue that the only real difference(s) between a disruption and a defining moment is our *place*, our *(dis)position,* and our *pursuit*. Our place is literally *where* we are at any given point in life. Our position (or disposition) is *how* we are at any given point. The two are very different, as we will observe below. Our pursuit is simple – where are we trying to end up?

Oftentimes our problem lies in thinking that any one of these are negotiable. Our place, position, and pursuit act as a three-legged stool; remove any one of these, and we will land flat on our face. You can even have a strong two, but without the third, there is no hope for victory in this race – no hope for making a defining moment that leads to destiny out of this disruption. Our epitaph would read like an old Luther Vandross song...

> I'm an ever-rollin' wheel, without a destination real
> I'm an ever-spinning top, whirling around till I drop
> Oh, but what am I to do, my mind is in a whirlpool
> Give me a little hope, one small thing to cling to

You got me going in circles!!!! Consider removing just one of these three necessary factors (place, position, pursuit), and there will always be delay, death, or derailment. **Place + Position – Pursuit = Stuck**. Without a destination, we would run aimlessly. An aimless run is not only counter-productive, but it is counter-Scripture. As we have already read – Paul warns against such running. Take the context of an Olympic runner. Imagine the personal and individual shame and embarrassment if an athlete worked so hard as to make the Olympic team, get to the starting line, heels on the running block, but at the firing of the pistol, runs as fast as they can across the lawn. Now imagine life, and the tendency to run without any aim. Where are we headed when our circumstances in life have hijacked our emotions? Where is the finish line when we are battling through things in life that seem to have robbed us of our very sanity? We must have an idea of where we are going if we are ever to make it there!

Just as the pursuit is critically important, imagine not being in position. **Place + Pursuit – Position = Bad Form**. Bad form doesn't just make the runner look bad but presents potential threats. *GQ* magazine reported several common runner's injuries, and notes that these can sometimes be a result of bad form.[107] Showing up at the starting line and identifying the finish line are pointless if you don't intend to run the right way! Our position is mostly our emotions…how we feel. Can you imagine an Olympic runner begin the 400M dash from a seated position, with their legs crossed, because that's what makes them most comfortable? It doesn't work that way! Why is it that we want life to work that way for us? What if forgiveness is the rule of the race? Some of us would rather suffer greater injuries caused by bitterness and hatred, simply because we don't feel like 'letting them off the hook.' Financial stewardship is the position that you ought to be in, but…YOLO, right? Delay, Death, Derailment!

Finally, **Position + Pursuit – Place = Straying**. Playing putt-putt golf with my children, when they were smaller, was quite interesting. They would step onto the course and place the ball where they thought they had the better chance of making it to the hole. That is what running this race without being in the right place is like. Keeping the image of the Olympian before us, imagine a runner deciding that they're going to start the race mid-way down the track, or from the stands, or anywhere else besides the starting line. It doesn't matter if they cross the line first or not – it's not a win because they didn't start from where they were supposed to. I am guilty of it and I am sure that you can relate as well! Far too often, we just want to take off running without knowing where we are. We might have all the right words.

---

[107] https://www.gq.com/story/5-most-common-running-injuries

From the outside looking in we may be doing all the right things. But because we missed the starting line, we're not even running the race we ought.

THERE'S NO 'PLACE' LIKE HOME!

Sometimes we struggle to find out where start is. Where exactly is my 'place?' It is probably not hard to understand that home is a great place to start. Even when our disruptions might be work related, ministry related, or a global pandemic, just taking the time to survey where things are in our private life will shine light on other areas in our life. I can tell you, I missed it – big time! Karen and I had our three boys, and thought that was it for us, but time had passed, and Karen really wanted a girl! She is the oldest of seven children in a single-mom household. Her late brother Neil was the only boy. You could imagine the culture-shock living with a husband and three growing boys! I alluded to the story, earlier, but let me tell you the expanded version.

Our youngest son, Jeremiah, was 9 years old when we decided that we wanted to give it one more try for a little girl. In fact, the more we talked about it, the more I was excited about having another child – especially a girl! I was older and more mature. We were doing better financially than when we had the boys, so let's do it! We began trying and praying. It took some time, but I will never forget the day Karen told me she was pregnant! I was not quiet about it! The boys were all surprise babies. This was the first time that we prayed specific prayers for a baby. Karen prayed for a girl…I prayed for twin girls! I even found ways to slip into my sermons the fact that we were having twin girls. I purchased twin girl accessories and ultrasound frames, and had twin girl names picked out! I was on my way to becoming #TwinGirlDad

Karen was nearing the end of her first trimester, and we went in for an ultrasound. They took the measurements, as we shared stories about being homeschooling parents of three boys. After the measurements, the doctor turned on the audio and we heard the precious little heartbeat. A rapid little thing, it was! I must be honest; I was disappointed at first that there weren't two heartbeats. I wanted TWO girls. That is what I had prayed for. It seemed God had other plans. Oh well, I'll take one… just make her twice as cute, God! Then the disruption came! After all our talking, laughing, measuring, and listening, the doctor sat us down and told us that she did not like the sound of the heartbeat. It was not beating at the rhythm that they would have wanted to hear. She handed us a pamphlet for coping with a miscarriage, 'just in case baby doesn't make it.'

Immediately, Karen broke down in tears. I held her hand tightly and told her not to worry! See, as I told the doctor, we have been praying for this child! We asked God for a baby girl, and we believed that God was a good, good father, and that he would grant us this request. I wasn't even hung up on the twin factor (secretly…or not so secretly, Karen did not want twins). Simply put, our pursuit was clear! This was a defining moment…we were having a girl…PERIOD! The more I spoke, the more I could feel my faith energized. I was in position, for sure! I even handed the pamphlet back to the doctor and assured her that we'd be back to share with her the good news about our healthy baby girl. This weakened heartbeat will not end in death, but in God receiving the glory, on account of our faith! *Preach, preacher!*

A month later, we went in for Karen's second ultrasound. In typing these words, I find myself unable to hold in the tears that stream down my face. The scene was but one of a few scenes that all converge together over a period of weeks as I recall the time when God called our precious baby home! Karen lay, for what seemed to be hours… silently, as the doctor scanned and pressed from every angle. This time, the monitor was not turned our way. No measurements to share. No conversations about big brothers and homeschool. Not even a complaint about a weakened heartbeat…there was no heartbeat. Our little answered prayer had gone to be with Jesus. What was an answered prayer became a disruption! I had questions for God – many of them. I did not even know where to start. I was in Bible college at the time, but neither the theological training of the academy, nor my spiritually vibrant church community offered solace to what I was dealing with inside. My poor wife; she seemed unable to escape the emotional maze of 'Why Lord?!' So, what happened? *On your mark, get set, go!*

I was set to go (position, pursuit), but I had never gotten on my mark (place). I altogether ignored the reality of what my family may go through. The reality is my faith-filled position (God will heal and deliver) was really my fearful disposition (I don't know what I will do if God doesn't heal and deliver). The reason for my disposition was that I never really considered my place. I hadn't looked at our circumstances through a medical lens nor a spiritual lens, simply an emotional one. Medically speaking, the heartbeat was irregular. Although to my untrained ear it was loud and fast, to the medically trained ear, that heartbeat would statistically not make it another month. There was no surgery or doctor's orders that could change that. I do not suggest that God could not have performed a biological miracle. I do recognize that I was not even in a place to truly appreciate it, if he did. Spiritually speaking, Karen and I were still the workmanship of God, even if a miscarriage was something that we would have to walk through, on our way to the 'good works.' I missed that.

Because I was not in the place where I should be (on my mark), I missed an opportunity to minister to my family. While it may look like I was strong in my faith because I refused the brochure on miscarriages, it reveals how weak my faith was. I believed that he could heal our baby's weak heart, but not our broken heart if the baby did not survive. My denial of 'what might be' robbed me of the opportunity to consider both science and Scripture, and understand what might be required of me if our child did not make it to term. How would I usher my wife back to a place of restored hope and faith in God? How would I ensure that my sons knew that this was not an indicator that God can't heal?

I missed that moment, but didn't even realize it until several months later. Time had passed, and the emotions of everything had caught up with me. I realized that I had simply weathered the initial trauma of everything, and moved right along with ministry, school, and work. I remember feeling so disappointed that I had not been more prepared to lead my family through one of the darkest seasons of our lives. Imagine our surprise when Karen found out 8 months later that she was pregnant again! Now imagine how distraught we were when we lost the second baby about 9 weeks later. This time was different, although for Karen it was exponentially more painful. I'll never forget her looking at me in the hospital, and asking how God could let this happen... TWICE.

At this time, I was in my second semester at Moody Theological Seminary. It was only by God's design that I would be in an apologetics class then. I had to answer whether I ever struggled believing in God, and why. This time the miscarriage was a defining moment, not simply a disruption. I prayed, I researched, I engaged in theological conversations (had to feed the nerd in me) and spoke with people who had experienced miscarriages. I started with where I was. I knew where Karen was. It wasn't until the place had firmly been established that I knew where I needed to be, in order to help Karen to where she needed to be. By God's grace, many conversations, some emotional long drives, and prayer, we both found ourselves trusting in God again, and I even began to pray once more for a little girl (still secretly wanted twins)!

Just about a year later, Karen was pregnant once again! When we heard the heartbeat at the first ultrasound, we burst into tears. When we found it was a girl at the second, more tears. At the third ultrasound, when the baby seemed to wave her hand, we sobbed…God never fails! And I guess I might as well mention that two years after Kennedy was born, God gave me my second little girl, Kharis…God never fails! Just for laughs, I prayed for twin girls, and although all my sons look like their mom, and even share many of her personality traits, the girls look and act like daddy (they love to talk, sing, and read books in their little library)! I guess I got my twins, but not the way I was expecting.

FROM THEORY TO APPLIED THEOLOGY

We now turn our attention to Scripture, to see how this all works out. Otherwise, it is merely inspirational dialog. Peter is a great teacher in this regard. We learn from the book of James that our disruptions have potential for great benefit. We are instructed by the apostle to count our trials as joy because they are instrumental in the development of our faith. When our faith is built through the endurance of these trials, James says that we become 'perfect and complete, lacking nothing' (James 1:2-4). Perfect and complete means that a developed faith leads to maturity. He further instructs that if we struggle in this area, that we are to seek wisdom from God through prayer. If James gives us a lesson in TRIALS 101, Peter takes it to another level in TRIALS 102.

> **James 1:2–5 (NASB)**
>
> [2] Consider it all joy, my brethren, when you encounter various trials, [3] knowing that the testing of your faith produces endurance. [4] And let endurance have *its* perfect result, so that you may be perfect and complete, lacking in nothing. [5] But if any of you lacks wisdom, let him ask of God, who gives to all generously and without reproach, and it will be given to him.

> **1 Peter 1:6–9 (NASB)**
>
> [6] In this you greatly rejoice, even though now for a little while, if necessary, you have been distressed by various trials, [7] so that the proof of your faith, being more precious than gold which is perishable, even though tested by fire, may be found to result in praise and glory and honor at the revelation of Jesus Christ; [8] and though you have not seen Him, you love Him, and though you do not see Him now, but believe in Him, you greatly rejoice with joy inexpressible and full of glory, [9] obtaining as the outcome of your faith the salvation of your souls.

Both James and Peter are writing to the same group of people. Though decades apart, the circumstances are the same – they are writing to believers on a journey. At this place in their journey, they find themselves scattered and not in the most favorable circumstances (see the opening greetings in their letters). James offers instruction on position – in our disruptions, joy should be our disposition. In Peter's letter, it seems as though he is applauding their position, but coaching them through the other vital parts of the race, place and pursuit. Joy, patience, matured faith, wisdom; these are all great, and necessary positions for us to be in, but so much more is needed.

James says, 'Consider what good can come out of this, and ask God if you need a little help in that regard.' Peter says, 'Look at where you are – a *temporary* place of necessary disruption. Great, you've learned to consider what good can come out of it, but don't focus on the gold medal that is a mature faith – no, the proof of that faith is much more valuable! Look beyond maturity to eternity! That is your pursuit!' What we learn from Peter is that our eschatological view (our beliefs about life after death) inform our ultimate view of disruptions. He goes on to explain further:

> **1 Peter 1:13 (NASB)**
>
> [13] Therefore, prepare your minds for action, keep sober *in spirit,* fix your hope completely on the grace to be brought to you at the revelation of Jesus Christ.

The rules for running the race, that can turn our disruptions into defining moments, are summed up in this short but powerful verse! Peter instructs his readers to get in the right place, to have the right disposition, and clarifies for them what the right pursuit must be. In the final stretch of this book, I want to walk through this verse, like we did with Ephesians 2:10. Are you ready to make a defining moment out of your disruption?

ON YOUR MARK | GETTING IN PLACE

The King James translation of this verse sounds rather humorous... *'therefore, gird up the loins of your mind...'* but it is rightly worded nonetheless. Gird, prepare, ready...the word choice may change, but each carries well the sentiment of what Peter is implying; getting in place starts in the head. The word that we read as gird up, prepare, or ready (ἀναζώννυμι | anazōnnymi) is a word that precedes action. It is not a daydreaming word, or Willy Wonka type of thought pattern, *'Come with me and you'll be in a world of pure imagination.'* Peter suggests that getting in place necessitates an expectancy of activity. Far from a defeated mindset that says, 'this is the end,' getting on our mark is a mindset that says, 'This is where I am but it is just the beginning...I am not supposed to stay here!' Why is this such an important place to start? It is because disruptions tend to knock us off course, especially mentally, from that which we have set out to do.

Think back to some of the disruptions that you have faced. What is the first thing that came to your mind? *Is this really happening to me right now?! How on earth did I get here?! This is so unreal!!* Or maybe the thoughts are far more elaborate. Karen and I have been homeschooling parents for eight years now. We've grown used to it, but I will never forget the onslaught of social media posts from parents all over the country when the Coronavirus pandemic caused schools nationwide to close.

> *Wait a minute, I did not go to school to be a middle school teacher!*

> *We did math differently when I was a kid – how am I supposed to teach my children?*

It broke my heart to see some pastors close the doors of their churches...

> *It was hard enough for me to prepare sermons for people who sat right in front of me, now I must preach online*

where the whole world can see? Will my own members even want to watch me instead of ...?

I can relate to these types of questions! All of us have gone through a disruption that caused us to ask questions. If we dig deeply, we will find that these are place questions. Do we have the strength and the resources to navigate from here? I say, 'Yes! Ask away!' Questions of place are not only healthy, but necessary! No one tries to navigate with a GPS without first establishing their current location! When we are in a shopping plaza, and looking for that certain store, it matters not where that store is located if we have not located that star on the map, signifying '*You are here*'. The truth is, we often have trouble navigating our disruptions simply, because we are in the wrong place.

Do you know someone who seemed to just give up? Do you know someone who just stopped trying? Perhaps it is because every attempt seemed to result in failure. As inspiring as the adage may sound, *'If, at first, you don't succeed...try, try again!'* the reality is that if you are 'trying' from the wrong place, you are destined to fail! Some have tried to rebuild without first removing! Some have made great efforts to strategize without first severing. You get the picture; getting in place is not just a matter of planning, but it is most certainly preparing! Imagine trying to build the 9/11 World Trade Center Memorial in NYC without removing all the debris that came from the devastating event! Just as problematic would be someone trying to rebuild a failed business without first undoing some of the destructive systems and practices that hurt the business in the first place.

I am not suggesting that every failed business is a result of neglect – there is a myriad of things that determines a business's success, including supply and demand, economy, or even a global pandemic. However, without stopping to ask, '*Where am I?*', the owner of a failed business would not know the true reason why their business failed. It is far easier to write it off to one of the above noted causes, instead of inspecting and finding out if one of these things (supply, demand, pandemic, etc.) exposed some areas of the business that needed attention. Even better – they may have revealed an opportunity to meet newly emerging needs. Such was the case for many cider mills and distilleries, who switched (even if temporarily) to producing large quantities of hand sanitizer in 2020. Quite an alternative to permanently closing doors.

What about relational disruptions? Maybe something has disrupted your family relationships. Instead of working on your marriage or your relationship with a parent, sibling, or a child, you want to move on to the next relationship without repairing the broken one. Maybe there are toxic people in your life that have set themselves up as permanent fixtures in your social circle. As a result, they are costing you healthy relationships. You have to ask yourself where your relational 'star on the map' is. Where are you? Pastor Michael Todd, of Transformation Church, often says in his sermons, 'God will not bless who you pretend to be.' I am inclined to agree with that suggestion, and add to it that he will not move you beyond *where* you pretend to be. Where are you?

Our starting point must be a prepared mind. The word (ἀναζώννυμι | anazōnnymi) means a binding up of the pants or garments so that one could walk unencumbered. Loose, flowing clothes would slow movement and prolong the journey. It is not an action word in and of itself, but rather a word that considers what must be done for movement to take place. Figuratively, when speaking of 'girding the mind,' we are ultimately talking about a place – a definitive starting point. We confess to have faith in God, yet yield to thoughts that are contrary to his will and purpose for our lives. That's a space from which we will not be able to successfully navigate life, especially through disruptions. John Eckhardt explains that this is what it means to be double-minded, and suggests that "[t]he majority of double-minded people manage to function in life and have some successes, yet they still have the characteristics of a spirit of schizophrenia. This causes them to be constantly unstable in every area, never having any peace about who they are or what they can or have to accomplish."[108] Does this sound familiar?

Long before Eckhardt, Jesus addressed this issue of the mind that is opposed to the will of God, and connected it to a matter of 'place.' The Gospels (Matthew 16; Mark 8) record Jesus telling his disciples about his soon-coming betrayal and ultimate crucifixion. It is no coincidence that the disciple who Jesus reprimands for an ungirded mind would be the one to write to believers, 'gird up the loins of your mind.' Peter was not really digging what Jesus was saying…'I left my fishing business to change the world with you – you think I would let someone try and take you out?! Over my dead body!' Jesus' rebuke was crystal clear! In both passages (Matthew

---

[108] John Eckhardt, *Unshakeable*, First edition. (Lake Mary, FL: Charisma House, 2015), 3.

16:23; Mark 8:33) Jesus says to Peter, 'Get behind me...you are not setting your mind on God's interests, but on man's.' To paraphrase, Jesus was in essence saying, 'You are in the wrong place – and it has everything to do with your thinking.' So often, we say that phrase, 'Get thee behind me, Satan!' without seriously making the connection that Jesus was confronting thought patterns, not a physical space.

We must understand the significance of this encounter, as it will help us to fully understand the next step (getting in position). Peter instructs that we are to gird, ready, or prepare our minds for action. But to be clear, he is speaking of a particular action as indicated by 'therefore.' The action for which we are preparing is predicated on the hope that we have in Jesus, beyond this temporary suffering. Therein lies the problem. Just like Peter, in the Gospels, we often prepare our mind for action, but it is not action based on the plan and purpose of God, but our own. We prepare our minds for agenda, not action. We prepare our mind for happiness. We ready our mind for a solution to our loneliness. We gird up our mind for an escape from our current conditions. We start from a place of 'me,' not a place of surrender to the one who has prepared our work in advance. Is it no wonder that when Jesus teaches the disciples to pray, he conveys, so early on, 'thy kingdom come, thy will be done...?'

Our mind must be ready only for the action(s) that will find us in the center of God's will! Getting in place means that we, like Paul, take every thought captive to the obedience of Christ (2 Corinthians 10:5). This practice of taking thoughts captive is not done by simply by sitting and engaging in thinking. While it might go without saying, some may be reading this chapter – 'thinking about thinking.' Preparing our mind is all about the organization and orientation of our thoughts. I offer three practical steps in preparing our mind for action; these three steps may move us to a more accurate starting point.

First, we must study the Word of God. In the Old Testament, the young leader Joshua is in a disruption of sorts. His mentor and leader just died. He has watched Moses lead this doubtful, fearful, rebellious nation for decades. He must now assume this leadership role. For many, this would be a promotion – and to be clear, it is. However, the circumstances were weighty, and the people were weightier! Promotions don't always mean peace! This promotion weighed heavy on his thoughts and emotions because God had to repeatedly tell Joshua to be strong and courageous, and not double-minded (Joshua 1:6-7). Finally, God gives him the recipe to obey such a command – meditate on the Word of God (Joshua 1:8). The command was not simply to read it or to memorize it – but to meditate on it, *day and night*. If we are going to prepare our mind, it must start with intentional, systematic time in God's Word. I dare not suggest that there is a specific number of verses, chapters, minutes, or hours that we should be reading daily...but we should be reading daily. We must read consistently and intentionally. For many of us, it is not the Word of God, but a social media feed, news report, or stock report that has our meditative space.

Second, something must be said of writing. Earlier, I noted how important journaling has been for me. It was an organic practice. I simply went to the study with my bible, a five-dollar journal, and a twelve-dollar pen. I would write out my prayers, because my mind had the tendency to roam – groceries, homeschool, work, squirrels, you name it. Eventually, I would write short commentary notes on passages that I was reading – questions, sermon titles, things to look up later. It was random and organic, but it worked for me. In seminary, I had to take a class on spiritual formation. There, journaling was a course requirement. I learned that devotional journaling was not something that I had just come up with – it is a rather ancient spiritual practice. More than a history lesson on journaling, I learned how rich a practice it can be, and various journaling methods.

Journaling looks quite different for me today! Although I have not quite adopted any method, there are pieces from different methods that I have added to my own regimen. I still write out my prayers, to a degree (or risk thinking about squirrels and shiny things), but so much more. I write down thoughts that come to mind as I am with the Lord. It might be people's names, it might be a song, it might be an answer to something I have been wrestling with. I also write down challenges, failures, disappointments, and more. Jack Hayford shares of his journal experience:

> I've also found it's wise to write down the bad things I am currently facing or being troubled by. If I write my problems down on paper, amazingly, I always find two things to be true. First, there weren't as many as I had thought. Second, when I write them down before the Lord, it seems as though the mere act of writing before Him both shrinks the threat of my problems and starts their solution. Right then, I will begin to sense direction and experience peace. There's something about defining those monsters on paper that moves them out of the fog of confusion and

turmoil. Writing them in the presence of Jesus gives perspective on *their* true size—and *His!* There's great power released through reflection and meditation in Christ's presence. Give time to it.[109]

One of the most important, consistent parts of the journaling experience is to note the day, time, and maybe even place which you are writing. Journaling is not simply about writing, but it is about recalling. One of the ways in which we prepare our mind for action is to recall past actions, good or bad; just as I had to think back to my failed readiness after our first miscarriage. Journaling enables us to look back and say, 'I was here once before! God brought me through this!' Or it helps us to see, 'I was here once before, and it brought me to ruin! I will not go in this direction again!' Writing helps us to take our thoughts captive to the plan and purpose of God. Writing is perhaps the most viable way to prepare our minds for action. God instructed Habakkuk to write the vision, so that the one who reads it may run with it (Habakkuk 2:2). We never know how time spent with the Lord might inform tomorrow's actions. I have written down things in my journal during my time with the Lord, things that I thought were random, that ended up being a catalyst for amazing conversation with my wife, or children, or a mentee later! You don't have to be an author, a blogger, or have good penmanship to journal, but it is one of the best ways for getting in place.

Finally, seek wisdom. Without wisdom, we are certain to encounter disruptions (Proverbs 13:10). Unfortunately, we live in a world where people prefer likes over listening. The problem is as old as time itself! The Bible tells of the Old Testament king, Rehoboam, who valued the advice of his peers who wanted to boost his ego, over the advice of his elders who wanted to see him rule long-term (1 Kings 12). The decision literally divided a nation. We cannot forget that someone has been where we are. We need people in our lives who are examples of Biblical living – people who we can process up to. We need people who can remind us, if need be, that our mind is 'not on God's interest, but on man's.'

Studying the Word, writing down our thoughts, seeking wisdom – this is what it means to prepare our minds for action. Let us not forget the context though – Peter wrote this to a people who were in the midst of a disruption, '…even though, for a little while… if necessary…' (1 Peter 1:6-

---

[109] Jack W. Hayford, *Living the Spirit Formed Life* (Ventura, CA: Regal; Gospel Light, 2001), 162.

9). The Word, writing, and wisdom – these are all practices in which we can engage, even during our disruptions. I don't suggest that any of these are easy in a disruption; in fact, they can be challenging even in the best of circumstances. The truth is, we live busy lives. Preparing our mind for action is something that takes intentional time. To prepare, we must pause. But in preparing our minds for action, we are finally in the right place to navigate the unexpected! We are ready to repurpose our disruption and make it a defining moment that leads to destiny!

GET SET | GETTING IN POSITION

Next, Peter instructs that we are to 'Keep sober in spirit.' The New Living Translation and the New Revised Standard Version both offer a great rendering of the word νήφοντες (nēphontes). While most translations render the word 'be sober,' these translations offer what the evidence of sobriety is – discipline, or self-control. The word does mean to be self-controlled, or well-balanced, being free from excess, passion, rashness, confusion, etc.[110] In other words, get ahold of yourself! Getting in *place*, as we discovered, is a matter of realization. It is an honesty moment – oftentimes, a humbling experience. Getting in *position* is a matter of response. Now that I am where I am supposed to be – my mind is prepared for action. *What do I need to do?*

We need not spend much time here, because the position(s) that we must get in will vary greatly, and there is no specific number of steps to getting set! It's kind of like the famous Nike slogan… Just do it! If you don't know what your 'it' is, that can be a good thing; it can be an indicator that you are not yet in the right place. By spending time in the word, reflective writing, and wise counsel, we are almost certain to know what 'it' we need to just do. While I cannot define your 'it,' I should offer clarity as to what 'it' is not. Remember, we are talking about getting in position, not taking off into our sprint, dash, or marathon. There is movement in the position, but the movement is only preparatory. Position movement is all about getting in the right state of readiness for the pulling of the trigger! It is getting high enough or low enough, making sure you are in a 'run-ready' posture. Although it sounds like preparing your mind, it is much more. You have already prepared your mind for action, now it is time for your actions to reflect the preparation.

---

[110] "νήφω," *BDAG, 672.*

You've seen the relay runners on the Olympics. They get up to the place where their run starts, but on the signal, they get their entire body in place, ready for that pistol to fire! That is what getting set is all about. You have been studying the Word, and journaling has become a part of your daily regimen. You have been meeting with a mentor, pastor, or elder in your life – asking some tough, revealing questions about the disruption you are going through. You are on your mark! What will it take for you to *get set*? The gun will eventually fire, and it will be time to move.

What does getting in position look like for you? Are you truly ready to take off running? Are you ready to run according to a new *modus operandi* (way of doing things)? Or do you plan on running the same way you did before all this took place? (Did someone say **DELAY!?**) Praying, journaling, wisdom processing – this all has to amount to a new mode of operation! Stride should change. Breathing control should improve. Posture and form should be more polished. What will it take to get in position? Do you need to sit down and write out a budget? Do you need to sit down and have that conversation that you have been avoiding? Do you need to schedule a meeting with a counselor – for you, or for your marriage? Maybe it is not that drastic. Perhaps getting in position for you means deleting certain distracting apps from your smartphone; cancelling certain entertainment subscriptions; or just turning off the television for a week to get the house in order. Are you ready to run!?

GO | GOING FOR THE PRIZE

And now the end draws near, and so we face the final curtain…*it's time to run!* But remember, we cannot run without a destination; doing so would certainly lead to delay, if not death or derailment! Everything that I have suggested previously reaches its head at this final point – our aim. In fact, Peter suggests as much in his writing of this verse. While it may seem as though Peter is giving three distinct commands here, *prepare, keep, fix* (NASB), he is giving only one command (fix your hope). The other verbs in this sentence (prepare, keep) are participles.

For those who (like me) haven't sat in an English class in a while, a participle is a verb that describes the condition of another verb. It is as if I were to say, 'Keeping all that you have just read in mind, embrace your disruption.' Ultimately, my instruction is that you embrace your disruption, but the way in which you embrace it is predicated upon you 'keeping…in mind.' Peter says to '…fix your hope completely on the grace to be brought to you at the revelation of Jesus Christ.' (NASB). The fixing of our hope is predicated upon our place and our position.

I will be the first to admit that what Peter instructs here is not always easy. We can sing songs and recite Scripture all day about having our hope fixed on Jesus, but Peter adds a little qualifier that messes the whole thing up. He says to fix our hope *completely* on the *grace* that is to be brought to us. We do not have to wait till the end of this chapter to engage in active discussion. Pause for a moment and think back to our pre-test. I asked you to identify the greatest three disruptions that you could remember. Now, answer this – what was the one thing that you desired the most in each of these? Honest answer. Here is one way to test the truth of your answer – what were you saying/doing the most during that disruption? Most of us, if truly honest, would admit that in our disruptions, we retreat to *'Are we there yet?'* mode. We look at our circumstances, only wishing to see the end, caring less about the destination, and more about the discomfort we are experiencing along the journey.

Where are you headed? What is the prize for which you are striving? For many, the goal is our happiness or comfort. *I can't wait till this is over, and life can go back to normal.* Do these words sound familiar? What if God did not want you to go back to what you called normal? The problem with happiness or comfort being the object of our hope is that these states of being are neither static nor permanent. I would not go as far as I have heard some say… 'God does not want us to be happy, but to be holy.' Yes and no. Absolutely, God desires us to be holy, but while happiness is not his ultimate desire for our lives, we would be gravely missing the heart of the Good Shepherd, who 'makes us lie down in green pastures,' (Psalm 23) if we were to suggest that he is not concerned with our happiness.

Happiness and comfort are fleeting things; they would serve as viable an option of salvation as an inflatable life raft in the middle of an ocean. They offer only temporary deliverance from what is, but they are neither designed to, nor hold the potential to offer a long-term solution. What we need, in the disruptions of life, is something that is anchored, static, sure, and not moved about with the winds and waves. What could be more concrete and immoveable than hope that is fixed on the grace that we have in God, through Christ? Consider how great a hope we have:

> **Romans 5:3–8 (NASB)**
>
> ³ And not only this, but we also exult in our tribulations, knowing that tribulation brings about perseverance; ⁴ and perseverance, proven character; and proven character, hope; ⁵ and hope does not disappoint, because the love of God has been poured out within our hearts through the Holy Spirit who was given to us. ⁶ For while we were still helpless, at the right time Christ died for the ungodly. ⁷ For one will hardly die for a righteous man; though perhaps for the good man someone would dare even to die. ⁸ But God demonstrates His own love toward us, in that while we were yet sinners, Christ died for us.

Our hope in Christ is the very source of our ability to navigate through disruptions. Remember, earlier we saw that disruptions are 'things,' and you might recall Paul's encouragement that all 'things' work together for the good of those who are called according to God's purpose. So, God causes disruptions to work together for our good, but what has this to do with hope? Looking at the greater context, we will see that it has much to do with hope!

> **Romans 8:24–28 (NASB)**
>
> ²⁴ For in hope we have been saved, but hope that is seen is not hope; for who hopes for what he *already* sees? ²⁵ But if we hope for what we do not see, with perseverance we wait eagerly for it. ²⁶ In the same way the Spirit also helps our weakness; for we do not know how to pray as we should, but the Spirit Himself intercedes for *us* with groanings too deep for words; ²⁷ and He who searches the hearts knows what the mind of the Spirit is, because He intercedes for the saints according to *the will of* God. ²⁸ And we know that God causes all things to work together for good to those who love God, to those who are called according to *His* purpose.

Hope and perseverance permeate Scripture. The more we hope, the more we persevere, and the more we persevere, the greater our hope! As we place our hope in Christ, the Holy Spirit is at work in the background. All of this comes back full circle to the very purpose and plan of God for our lives (... made for good works, that we might walk in them). What Paul is saying is that, as we place our hope in Jesus, we are strengthened to persevere. How are we strengthened? We do not see it on the surface – just as that which we hope for is unseen, but nonetheless very real! The Holy Spirit intercedes for us, in ways we could not even imagine – and his prayer is not our will, but the will of God... *and we know that God causes all things to work together....*! He is working them together because we have set our focus on the right prize. What is your prize? Hope that is directed toward the grace brought to us at the revelation of Jesus Christ (ultimately, holiness) must be our goal – leave happiness in the hands of God; remember, he's a good, good Father, and he is truly concerned for us!

Going for the prize is not just about focus, it is about patience! Just as a runner can be penalized for a false start, we often experience penalties for false starts in our disruptions. It's not that you were not supposed to start that business... just that no one said 'GO!' yet. It's not that you weren't supposed to marry that person...you just moved before the official gave the signal. Peter says that the grace on which we are to fix our hope has a proleptic distinction – it anticipates something that has not yet occurred. The goal is not simply the favorable end of our circumstances. The grace that Peter speaks of is an eternal grace that we have as believers. The hope we have in Christ makes every disruption that we face seem as though they really are – temporary. Considering eternity, what I am facing right now is but a fleeting moment. Sure, this is easier written than lived out, but it is nevertheless real.

The patience that this hope requires is a challenge to us because it is something that we cannot put on the calendar. I remember when I proposed to Karen – the night was beautiful and full of romance. The weeks to follow, however, felt like an eternity. For many reasons, including the fact that we were young and saving to pay for a wedding on our own, we did not have a date. Weeks turned into a couple of months, and I can remember wondering, are we going to be one of those couples who are engaged longer than we are even married? Maybe that is an exaggeration, but it just seemed like an eternity. We set a date in early December; but, having the date on the calendar made the next eight months seem shorter than the first two and a half. There is something about being able to set 'hope' on the calendar, but that is just not how our hope in Jesus works. James tells us to let patience have its perfect work (James 1:4). The results are a better version of you.

WHAT ARE YOU AIMING FOR?

Hope in Jesus and patience in the waiting – that is our pursuit…he is our prize. But how does this look, in a practical sense? Just as the Olympic runner is not running for the gold medal (that is just a token to commemorate the moment), we are not running through our disruption to get to financial freedom, a healthier marriage, a better job, or any other favorable outcome. We are running to obtain that which is set before us as a prize (the grace to be brought to us at the revelation of Jesus Christ). As we navigate through our disruption, we consult the Word of God, reflect on our journey through a journal of some sort, and process up to wise counsel. We are on our mark! Having reached the right place; that is, having our mind prepared for action, we act – we get in position. Whatever needs to be adjusted right now, we adjust. If it is an attitude adjustment, we adjust. If it is better financial stewardship, we budget and settle debts. If it is learning a love language in order to better steward our marriage – we are all in! We are in position. We do all of this so that we can run, and run well. Our pursuit is the grace that we have in Jesus – this is our finish line. Our finish line is much greater than this situation – it is eternity with Jesus. This finish line fuels our perseverance.

That is what makes our disruption become a defining moment: everything that Jesus has done, and that which is laid up for us, becomes the lens through which we view our circumstances, and the regulations by which we 'run the race,' that is, navigate our disruption(s). If happiness is your aim, you might achieve it, but only momentarily. Your disruption will end in delay. Our own happiness can sometimes be a very dangerous thing. Sometimes what may make us happy, leads to immoral decisions. James chapter 4 has much to say on this matter! If James is right in his suggestion that fights and quarrels come from our desires, and I believe that he is, then it means that pursuing happiness, or the 'favorable end' of our disruption could lead to more than simple delay, but also death and derailment. So, I ask again, *what are you aiming for?*

QUESTIONS FOR REFLECTION

1. I use the analogy of a race in this chapter to help you visualize navigating through a disruption into your destiny. I also offered an example of my own failed attempt to navigate through a disruption. What is the first necessary step for you to be 'on your mark'? What is at stake if you skip this step?

2. Now that you have identified your starting place, it's time to get in position to move. Peter says that self-control is the next step. What are some disciplines, or practices that moving forward in your destiny demands of you? Consider what the results might be if you neglect these disciplines or practices.

3. In this book, when I speak of destiny, I mean the destination that God has intended for us in our journey through life. How much thought did you give to what this intended destination might be prior to the disruption(s) you faced? How do hope and holiness factor into this intended destination?

4. How would keeping this intended destination in mind during the disruption(s) you have encountered help you navigate them better?

7 CONCLUSION: WHERE DO YOU START?

Friend, I hope to have provided you with the fuel that you need to navigate the unexpected 'hard times' in your life – not just the current one, but also future disruptions. Even though the last chapter seemed to lay out a very clear starting point, there is one more thing that I would like to bring light to. Aside from Jesus, there is probably no greater example of a person facing a disruption in the Bible than the man named Job. Job offers us a great note to end on, because here we find a man who is advanced in years and established in life. For some, perhaps even most reading this book, disruption is not a situation that you remember, but one that you are currently in. Who purchases a diet book after they have lost weight? The reality is, you are possibly facing a disruption, and have given every reason why yours is a hopeless case. Has God's Word failed? Indeed, it has not – it cannot. This truth came to Job, albeit late in his trials. This realization made all the difference in the world for his circumstances.

The entire book of Job reads as a disruption documentary. By the third chapter, Job is lamenting; crying out with words that sound uncomfortably familiar to anyone who has faced a disruption. He's cursing the day that he was born, questioning God…all the signs of someone headed for delay, death, or derailment. His wife is no help, his friends are certainly no help. As the narrative progresses, Job finds himself still believing in God, but shaking his fists at him, verbally. Sound familiar? The lesson, however, is in the final chapter. In chapter 40, Job basically tells himself to be silent! God will then speak in chapter 40 and 41. Job is reminded how infinitely greater God is than he. God basically says to Job, 'If you had my wisdom, power, and authority, then you would be able to save yourself…how's that working out for you?' In other words, 'I know what I am doing, so why are you questioning me?!' Job comes to himself in chapter 42.

> **Job 42:1–6 (NASB)**
>
> [1] Then Job answered the Lord and said, [2] "I know that You can do all things, And that no purpose of Yours can be thwarted. [3] 'Who is this that hides counsel without knowledge?' "Therefore I have declared that which I did not understand, Things too wonderful for me, which I did not know." [4] 'Hear, now, and I will speak; I will ask You, and You instruct me.' [5] "I have heard of You by the hearing of the ear; But now my eye sees You; [6] Therefore I retract, And I repent in dust and ashes

On your mark, get set, go! Job had to get his mind prepared for action (I *know* you can do all things…). After almost forty chapters of what Job *thought,* how he *felt*, and what he *preferred*, none of these led to a better Job, only a bitter one. His waiting, his speaking, and his thinking, all were things we can empathize with, but none that we should emulate. Job then brought his words and actions into subjection of his *readied* thoughts (*I will ask... and heed instructions*). Now having gotten into place and position, Job is finally ready to make his pursuit. His pursuit is restoration to God himself (*now, my eyes see you*), and true repentance (*I retract and repent*). Job's focus was no longer on his disruption, nor was it wrongly directed toward God. His focus was not on what he had lost or what God had 'taken away,' but it was on this God 'who can do all things,' and whose 'purpose cannot be thwarted.' Although Ephesians 2:10 and Romans 8:28 had not yet been written, the truths which they convey had become real for Job – God has a purpose (Ephesians) and disruptions do not interrupt that purpose but are part and parcel of them (Romans).

The lesson we have already learned – get in place, get in position, go for the prize. The lesson that we would do well to also learn is in the beginning of this passage – *then Job answered the Lord.* Place, position, and pursuit should be predicated on prayer – talking to God. Truly, what a friend we have in Jesus, all our sins and disruptions to bear; what a privilege it is to know that he is a God who answers prayer! It is not until the end of the Book of Job that we find him offering a *surrendered* prayer to God. Imagine how different the narrative might have read if this is how he began. What are you doing? This is the question that I proposed early in this book. We have learned to wait, and learned to speak life into our disruptions.

In order to avoid derailment, we learned to think Biblically about our circumstances; think rightly about God, his care, and his purpose for our life. Finally, we learned that our aim must not be mere happiness, nor the favorable end of our disruption, but our finish line is eschatological – it is eternity with Jesus. All else, even this pain, is temporary. All these doings: waiting, speaking, thinking, aiming, are great. Rightly aligned, they can lead us toward destiny – the maturing of our purpose. Without surrendered prayer (prayer that acknowledges and submits to God's power, purpose, and plan), they will quickly become frustrating endeavors. So, where do we start? We start with prayer.

I have encountered plenty more disruptions than the pages of this book allow for. I experienced disruptions in my childhood. My teenage years are replete with disruptions. As an adult, I have faced disruptions that almost brought me to ruin; disruptions that almost cost me my marriage, my job, and almost caused me to lose my mind. In almost every one of them, I did not have the tools to navigate them well. The delays are embarrassing. The deaths are high in number – thank God that he is the resurrection! I am amazed how God has miraculously rebuilt the people, purpose, and dreams that had been damaged in the wakes of derailments that I have caused for my inability to navigate the unexpected disruptions in my life the right way. I have written this book in hopes that the lessons that I have come to learn will equip and encourage you, as you navigate your unexpected disruptions. I would like to give one final suggestion, before we bring this book to a close. Using Ephesians 2:10 as our model, I offer the following prayer for you, in your disruption.

CLOSING PRAYER

Lord, with your hands, you have made me – a workmanship.
In Jesus, you have made me over.
Whatever distortions that sin and circumstances may have caused,
the blood of Jesus has cleansed.
Although my current circumstances do not seem to suggest as much,
I know that you have a purpose for my life!
This is not my end;
rather, it is part of the preparation that you have allowed,
in order to usher me into in my purpose – my destiny.
As I navigate this unexpected trial,
I ask that you give me the strength to wait on you, and you alone.
Help me, Lord, to speak life into my disruption – you are the resurrection!
May my thoughts be informed by and aligned with your Word.
Lord, I set my hope on the grace found only in you!
I am your workmanship, created in Christ Jesus, for good works!
You have prepared them, and I commit to walking in them.
In Jesus' name – Amen!

BIBLIOGRAPHY

Arndt, William, Frederick W. Danker, Walter Bauer, and F. Wilbur Gingrich. *A Greek-English Lexicon of the New Testament and Other Early Christian Literature*. Chicago: University of Chicago Press, 2000.

Bray, Gerald. *God Is Love: A Biblical and Systematic Theology*. Wheaton, IL: Crossway, 2012.

Bridges, Jerry. *Trusting God*. Colorado Springs, CO: NavPress, 1988.

Briley, Terry R. *Isaiah*. The College Press NIV Commentary. Joplin, MO: College Press Pub., 2000–.

Carson, D. A. *The God Who Is There: Finding Your Place in God's Story*. Grand Rapids, MI: Baker Books, 2010.

Chapman, Gary. *Covenant Marriage: Building Communication & Intimacy*. Nashville, TN: Broadman & Holman Publishers, 2003.

Clatworthy, Jonathan. *Making Sense of Faith in God: How Belief Makes Science Possible*. London: SPCK, 2012.

Comfort, Ray. *God Doesn't Believe in Atheists: Proof That the Atheist Doesn't Exist*. Orlando, FL: Bridge-Logos Publishers, 1993.

Dobson, James. *When God Doesn't Make Sense*. Wheaton, IL: Tyndale House, 1993.

Duffield, Guy P., and Nathaniel M. Van Cleave. *Foundations of Pentecostal Theology*. Los Angeles, CA: L.I.F.E. Bible College, 1983.

Eastman, Dick. *The Hour That Changes the World: A Practical Plan for Personal Prayer*. Grand Rapids, MI: Chosen, 2002.

Eckhardt, John. *Unshakeable*. First edition. Lake Mary, FL: Charisma House, 2015.

Ennis, Paul. *The Moody Handbook of Theology, Revised and Expanded*. Chicago, IL: Moody Publishers, 1989.

Frame, John M. *Christianity Considered: A Guide for Skeptics and Seekers*. Edited by Todd Hains, Mark L. Ward Jr., and Elizabeth Vince. Bellingham, WA: Lexham Press, 2018.

Goldsmith, Marshall. *What Got You Here Won't Get You There: How Successful People Become Even More Successful*. New York: Hachette Books, 2007.

Hayford, Jack W. *Hope for a Hopeless Day: Encouragement and Inspiration When You Need It Most*. Ventura, CA: Regal; Gospel Light, 2007.

———. *Living the Spirit Formed Life*. Ventura, CA: Regal; Gospel Light, 2001. Heywood, David. *Transforming Preaching: The Sermon as a Channel for God's Word*. SPCK Library of Ministry. London: SPCK, 2013.

Jobe, Mark, *UNSTUCK: Out of Your Cave, Into Your Call*. Chicago, IL: Moody, 2014.

Keller, Timothy. *The Reason for God: Belief in an Age of Skepticism*. New York: Penguin Books, 2009.

Keller, Timothy, and Katherine Leary Alsdorf. *Every Good Endeavor: Connecting Your Work to God's Work*. New York: Dutton, 2012.

Louw, Johannes P., and Eugene Albert Nida. *Greek-English Lexicon of the New Testament: Based on Semantic Domains*. New York: United Bible Societies, 1996.

Maxwell, John C. *Failing Forward: Turning Mistakes into Stepping-Stones for Success*. Nashville, TN: Thomas Nelson Publishers, 2000.

McGrath, Alister. *Why God Won't Go Away: Engaging with the New Atheism*. London: SPCK, 2011.

Messenger, William. "Introduction to the Theology of Work." In *Genesis through Revelation*, edited by William Messenger. Vol. 1–5. Theology of Work Bible Commentary. Peabody, MA: Hendrickson Publishers, 2014–2016.

Murray, Andrew. *The School of Obedience*. London: J. Nisbet & Co., 1898.

———. *Waiting on God! Daily Messages for a Month*. New York; Chicago; Toronto: Fleming H. Revell, 1896.

———. *Working for God!: A Sequel to Waiting on God!*. New York; Chicago; Toronto: Fleming H. Revell, 1901.

Myers, Allen C. *The Eerdmans Bible Dictionary*. Grand Rapids, MI: Eerdmans, 1987.

Ortberg, John. *The Life You've Always Wanted: Spiritual Disciplines for Ordinary People*. Grand Rapids, MI: Zondervan, 1997.

Piper, John. *Coronavirus and Christ*. Wheaton, IL: Crossway, 2020.

———. *When the Darkness Will Not Lift: Doing What We Can While We Wait for God—And Joy*. Wheaton, IL: Crossway Books, 2006.

Quinn, Benjamin T., and Walter R. Strickland II. *Every Waking Hour: An Introduction to Work and Vocation for Christians*. Bellingham, WA: Lexham Press; Southeastern Baptist Theological Seminary, 2016.

Robinson, Haddon. *Biblical Preaching: The Development and Delivery of Expository Messages*. Grand Rapids, MI: Baker Publishing Group, 1980.

Robinson, Haddon. "Chapter Four: Blending Bible Content and Life Application." In *Mastering Contemporary Preaching*. Portland, OR: Multnomah, 1989.

Shenk, David W. *Global Gods: Exploring the Role of Religions in Modern Societies*. Scottdale, PA: Herald Press, 1995.

Sherlock, Charles. *The Doctrine of Humanity*. Edited by Gerald Bray. Contours of Christian Theology. Downers Grove, IL: InterVarsity Press, 1996.

Sproul, R. C. *Surprised by Suffering: The Role of Pain and Death in the Christian Life*. Lake Mary, FL: Reformation Trust Publishing, 2010.

———. *What Can We Know about God?* First edition. Vol. 27. The Crucial Questions Series. Orlando, FL: Reformation Trust: A Division of Ligonier Ministries, 2017.

Stott, John. *Why I Am a Christian*. Nottingham, England: Inter-Varsity Press, 2003.

Thiselton, Anthony C. *Systematic Theology*. Grand Rapids, MI; Cambridge, U.K.: William B. Eerdmans Publishing Company, 2015.

Tozer, A.W. *The Root of the Righteous.* Camp Hill, Pennsylvania: Christian Publications, 1955.

Tucker, J. Brian. *Reading 1 Corinthians.* Eugene, OR: Wipf and Stock, 2017.

———. *Remain in Your Calling: Paul and the Continuation of Social Identities in 1 Corinthians.* Eugene, OR: Pickwick Publications, 2011.

Tucker, J. Brian and John Koessler. *All Together Different. Upholding the Church's Unity While Honoring Our Individual Identities.* Chicago, IL: Moody Publishers, 2017.

VanGemeren, Willem, ed. *New International Dictionary of Old Testament Theology & Exegesis.* Grand Rapids, MI: Zondervan Publishing House, 1997.

Wallace, Daniel B. *Greek Grammar beyond the Basics: An Exegetical Syntax of the New Testament.* Grand Rapids, MI: Zondervan, 1996.

Wiersbe, Warren W. *Be Comforted.* "Be" Commentary Series. Wheaton, IL: Victor Books, 1996.

Wilson, Jim L. and Earl Waggoner. *A Guide to Theological Reflection: A Fresh Approach for Practical Ministry Courses and Theological Field Education.* Grand Rapids, MI: Zondervan Academic, 2020.

Wright, N. T. *Following Jesus: Biblical Reflections on Discipleship.* London: Society for Promoting Christian Knowledge, 1994.

———. *Simply Christian.* London: Society for Promoting Christian Knowledge, 2006.

Zackery, Curtis. *Soul Rest: Reclaim Your Life; Return to Sabbath.* Edited by Abigail Stocker, Justin Marr, Lynnea Smoyer, and Christy Callahan. Bellingham, WA: Kirkdale Press, 2018.

ABOUT THE AUTHOR

Aaron j Robinson (AaronjRob) is an urban pastor, scholar, and teacher. A recognized leader in the local church, Aaron began serving in ministry leadership in the late nineties. He has served in several ministry leadership positions, such as children and youth ministries, worship, media, and pastoring at the executive associate level. He currently serves as Spiritual Life Director and Chief Operations Officer of the Power Company Kids Club - a ministry that serves over 1,000 children, youth, and their families in Detroit and Pontiac, Michigan every week.

His work as a media director in the local church served as a catalyst to launching a digital media firm, which served the media and communication needs of churches and faith-based 501c3 organizations. Through his business, Aaron has been privileged to work with great ministries, from local churches and community development organizations to national and international ministries, such as Compassion International, World Vision, and The Brooklyn Tabernacle.

In 2018, Aaron graduated Summa Cum Laude from Moody Theological Seminary, with a Master of Divinity degree, with a focus in pastoral studies. Aaron is currently completing his PhD in Theology (New Testament) through the University of Bangor, in Wales, UK (Centre of Pentecostal and Charismatic Studies). His research embodies his passion and ministry experience - the faithful witness of the local church (based on a reading of the book of Revelation). Aaron's deep appreciation for theology comes from his diverse experience in theological education, having formally studied in both Reformed and Pentecostal/Charismatic universities.

Aaron and Karen have been married for 22 years. They live in the metro-Detroit community where they minister. They are proud parents of five children; Aaron II, Isaiah, Jeremiah, Kennedy, and Kharis.

www.ingramcontent.com/pod-product-compliance
Lightning Source LLC
Chambersburg PA
CBHW060537100426
42743CB00009B/1554